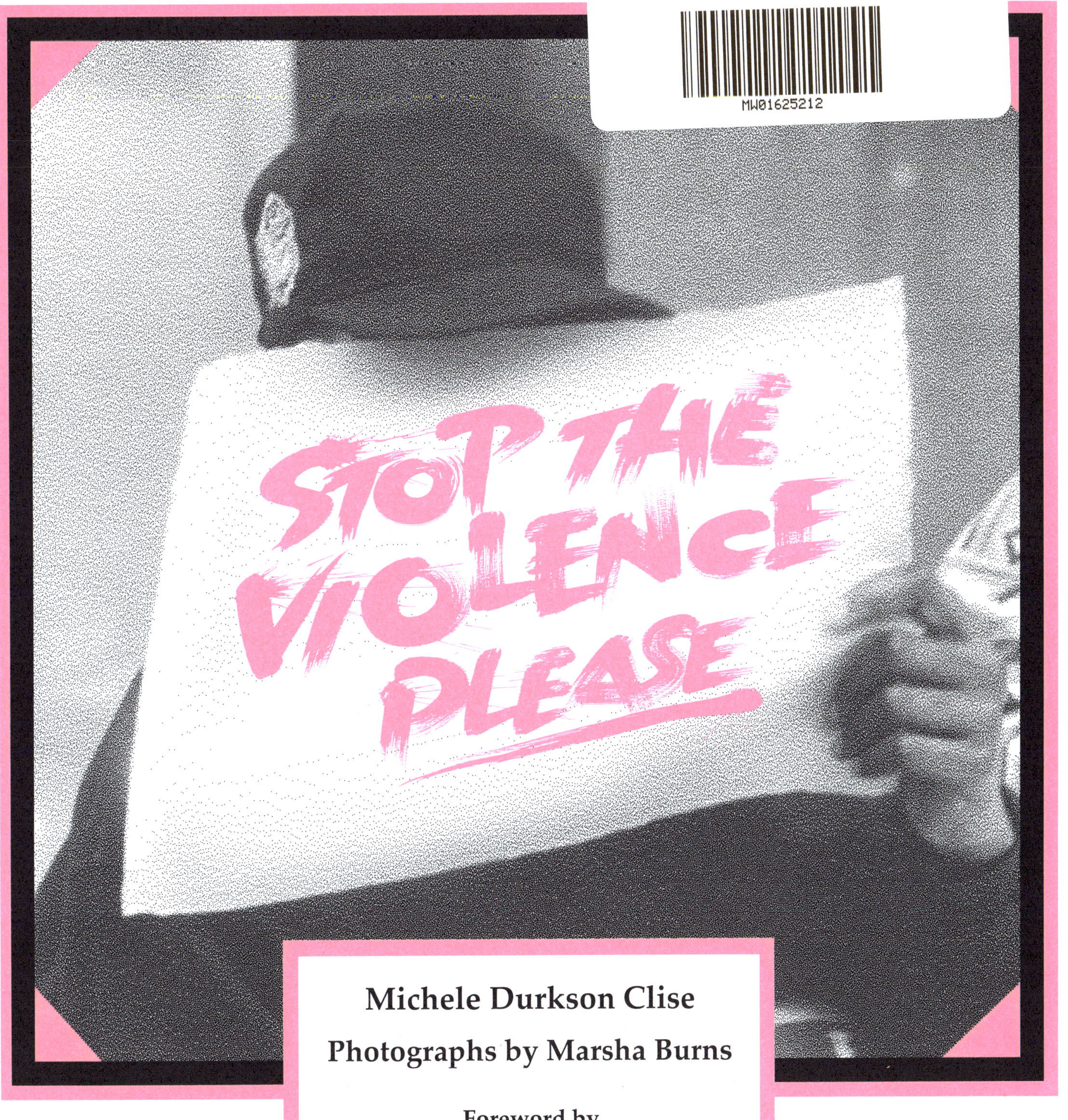

MW01625212

Michele Durkson Clise

Photographs by Marsha Burns

Foreword by
Judge Michael Salvador Hurtado

Allied Arts Foundation
in association with
University of Washington Press

Seattle

Ah! What would the world be to us
If the children were no more?

Henry Wadsworth Longfellow

Copyright © 1994 by Michele Durkson Clise

All rights reserved. No part of this publication may be reproduced or transmitted in any form or by any means, electronic or mechanical, including photocopy, recording, or any information storage or retrieval system, without permission in writing from the publisher.

Library of Congress Cataloging-in-Publication Data
Clise, Michele Durkson.
Stop the violence please / Michele Durkson Clise ;
photographs by Marsha Burns ; foreword by Michael Salvador Hurtado.
p. cm.
Includes bibliographical references.
Summary: While playing with a gun, a teenager accidentally kills two children. Includes facts about gun violence, steps that parents and children can take to stop the violence, and a list of related books, films, and organizations.
ISBN 0-295-97367-6 (alk. paper)
[1. Violence--Fiction. 2. Firearms--Fiction. 3. Gun control--Fiction.]
I. Burns, Marsha, ill. II. Title.
PZ7.C62284 1994
[Fic]--dc20

The paper used in this publication meets the minimum requirements of American National Standard for Information Sciences—Permanence of Paper for Printed Library Materials, ANSI Z39.48-1984.

Cover illustration by Tim Girvin Design and the "Live and Direct Kids" from Atlantic Street

Photographs are by Marsha Burns unless noted otherwise.

Distributed by University of Washington Press,
P.O. Box 50096, Seattle, WA 98145-5096

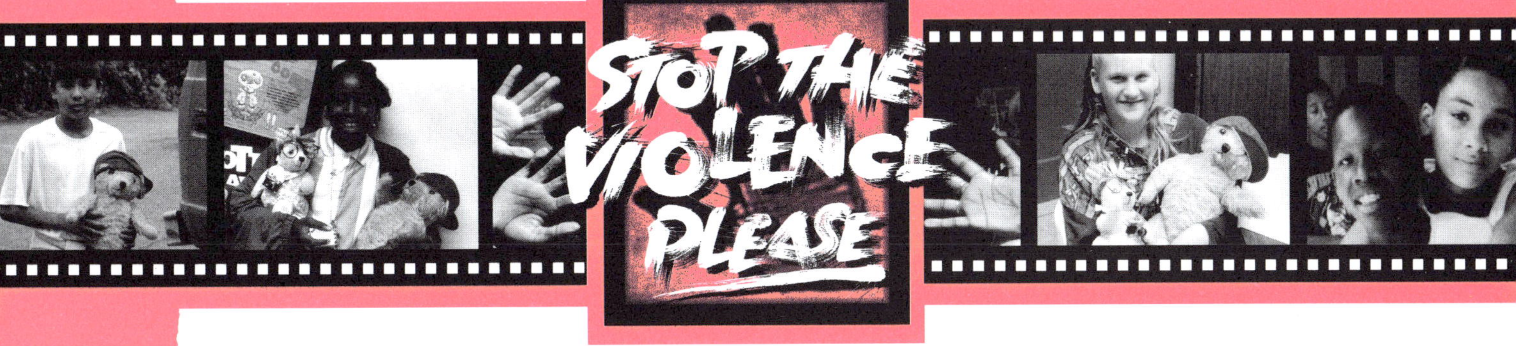

Contents

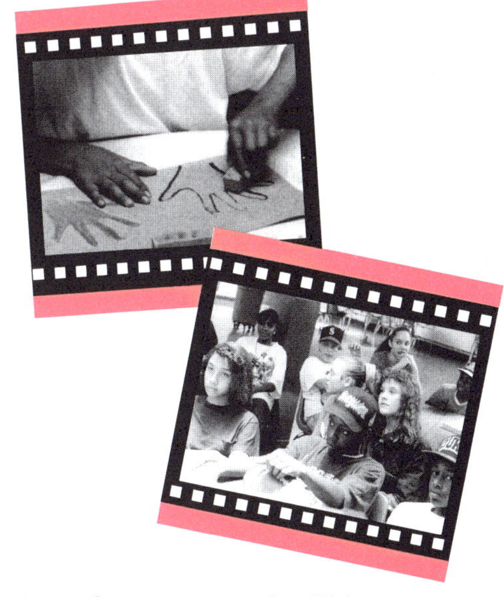

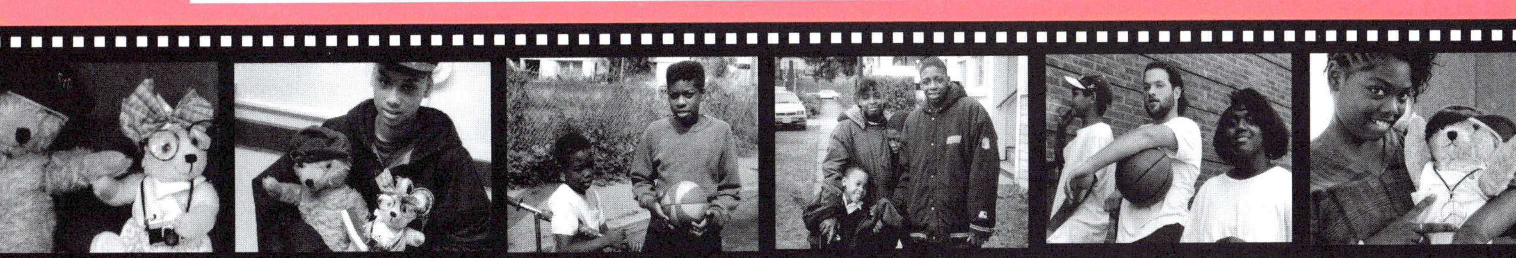

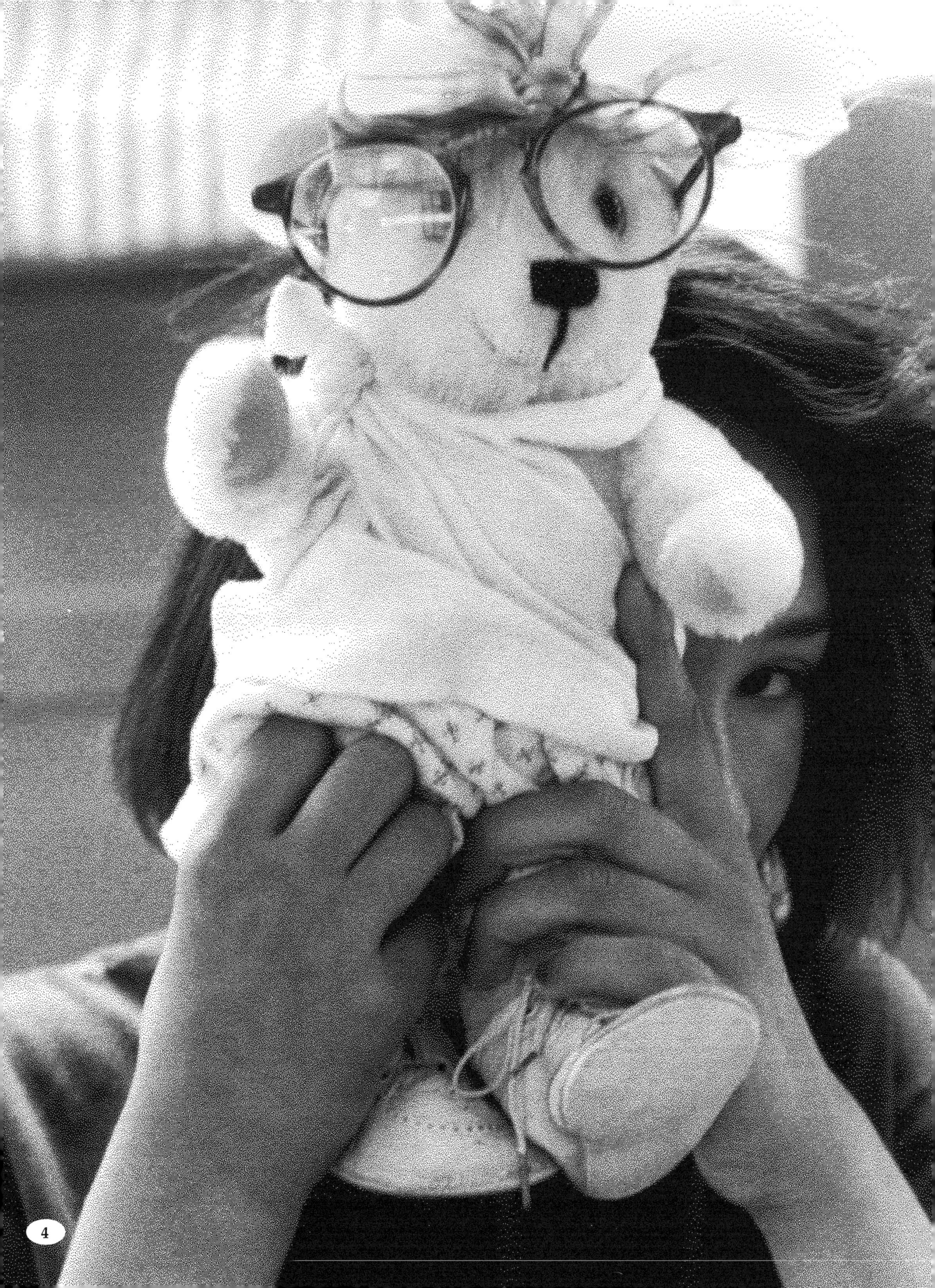

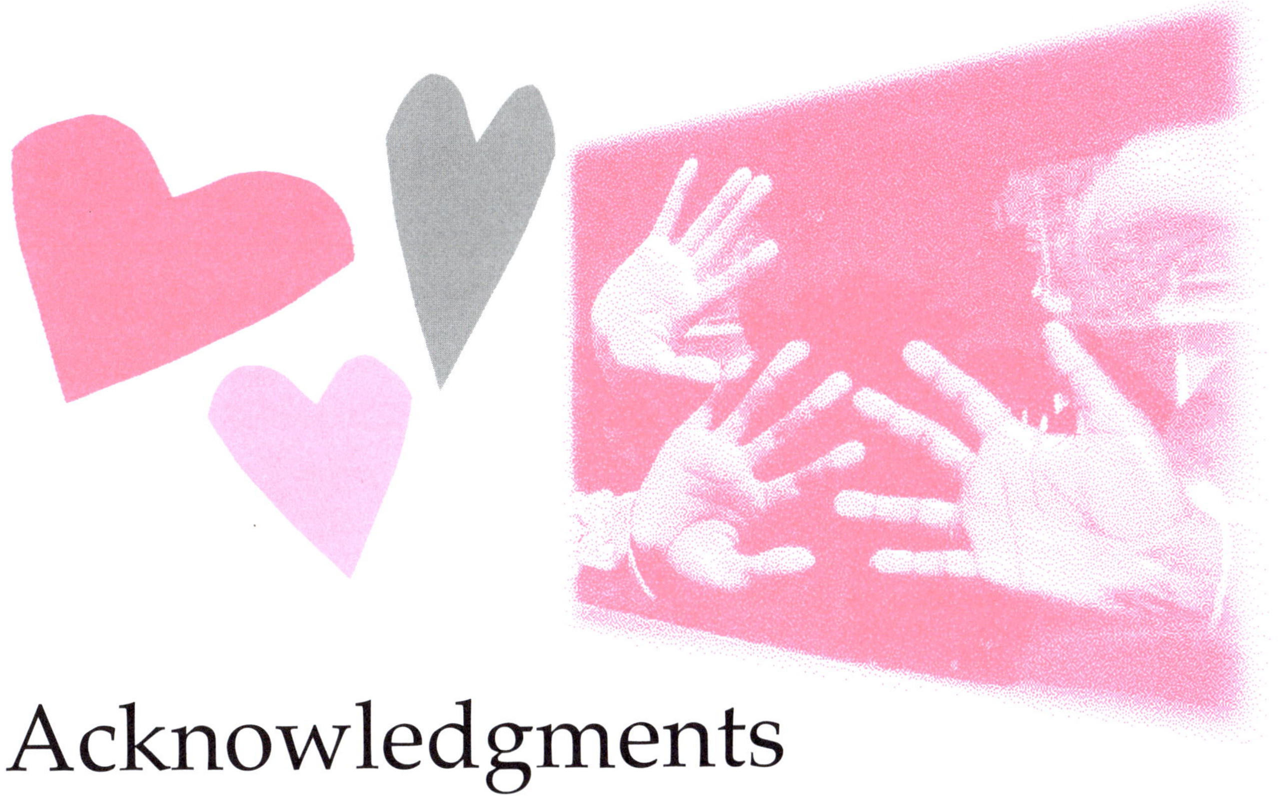

Acknowledgments

The more I became involved with the issue of children and gun violence, the more I wanted to know. I read many books and viewed films and videos. Included in the "Reading List, Films, Organizations, and Resources" section of this book are the ones I found to be the most informative and challenging. They tell it like it is.

I made every effort to speak to others involved in the same arena. The Seattle Police Department's Gang Intervention Unit and Homicide Division, as well as several members of the ERT (Emergency Response Team) provided invaluable insight.

The Office of the Mayor of Seattle and members of the city Justice Department and judicial system made it possible for me to participate in some of their efforts to stop the violence.

The staff at Harborview Medical Center generously guided me to literature and sources of facts and statistics. The Puget Sound Blood Center also provided valuable information.

There is not enough room to mention all of the community activities, organizations, and grass roots groups involved with youth and social justice, but I have included in the list of organizations a selection for readers who want to become involved. Whether it be through one of these organizations or through an idea that you develop, I encourage each and every reader to reach out and help.

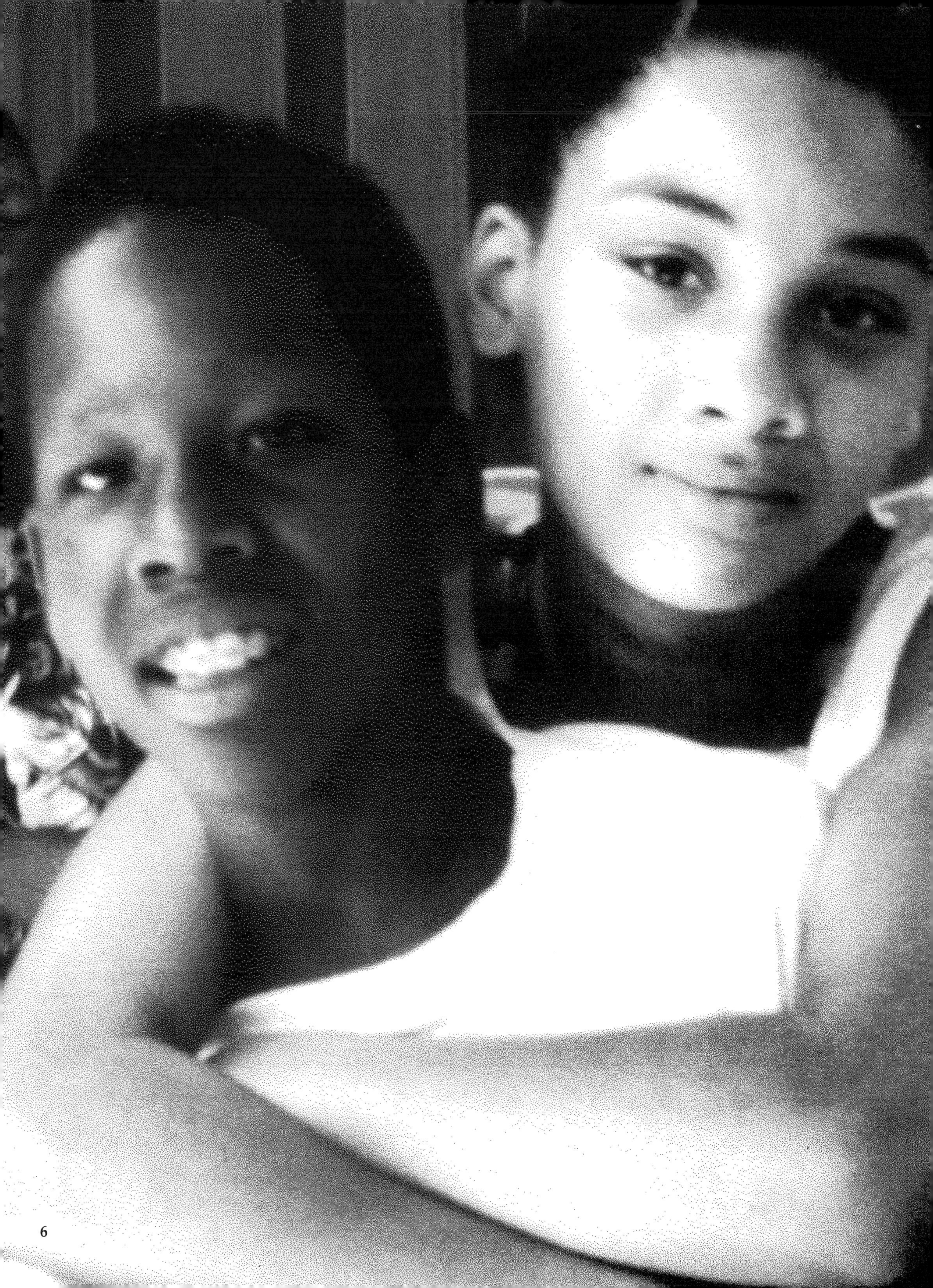

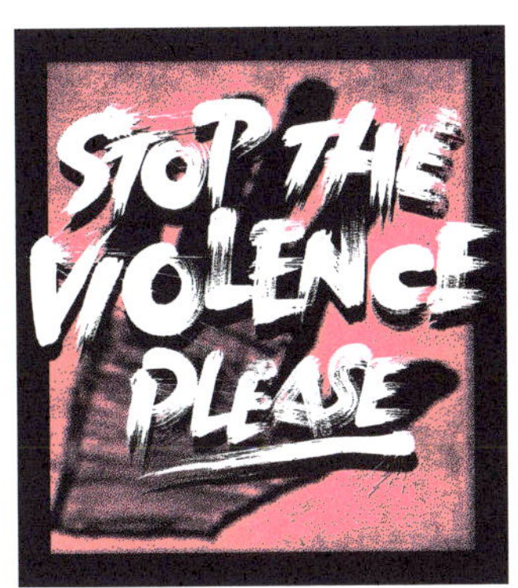

Foreword - A Message from the Heart

The reader of this book cannot help but find the presentation thoughtful and direct. As you read the text and ponder the photographs, I hope that you will be sharing your impressions, emotions, and yes, outrage, with someone you love. Until we, as a society, can face up to the ugly truth that violence and guns are killing our children at levels never before imagined, the scourge will continue.

The answer to this dilemma, I believe, lies within the human spirit to survive. I do not mean to oversimplify the issue, but only to highlight the obvious—that we have the ability to chart our own destiny. What we do, or don't do, within this generation will have a profound effect on generations to come. One need only look at the faces of the children on the pages of this book and be reminded that the burden of change falls on you and me. Change, like love, takes courage, but to create the change that is needed takes both love and courage.

Being a judge in one of the busiest courtrooms in Seattle gives me standing to sound the alarm. The people who appear in my court are considered "adults." They are all too often beyond alarm. Therefore, we must focus our efforts on the very audience that causes the alarm—our children.

Violence and guns are accepted by many as the price for "livin' in the city" and "livin' in America." We must not accept these attitudes. The price is too high.

Look at the faces of the children in this book. Put it down, go to the mirror, and look at the face of the only person who can possibly do anything about paying "the price." Then ask, "Are you willing to pay?"

I wish to thank Michele for this opportunity to speak from my heart. I hope you will share this book with family and friends, join the effort to save our children, and increase the peace.

Judge Michael Salvador Hurtado

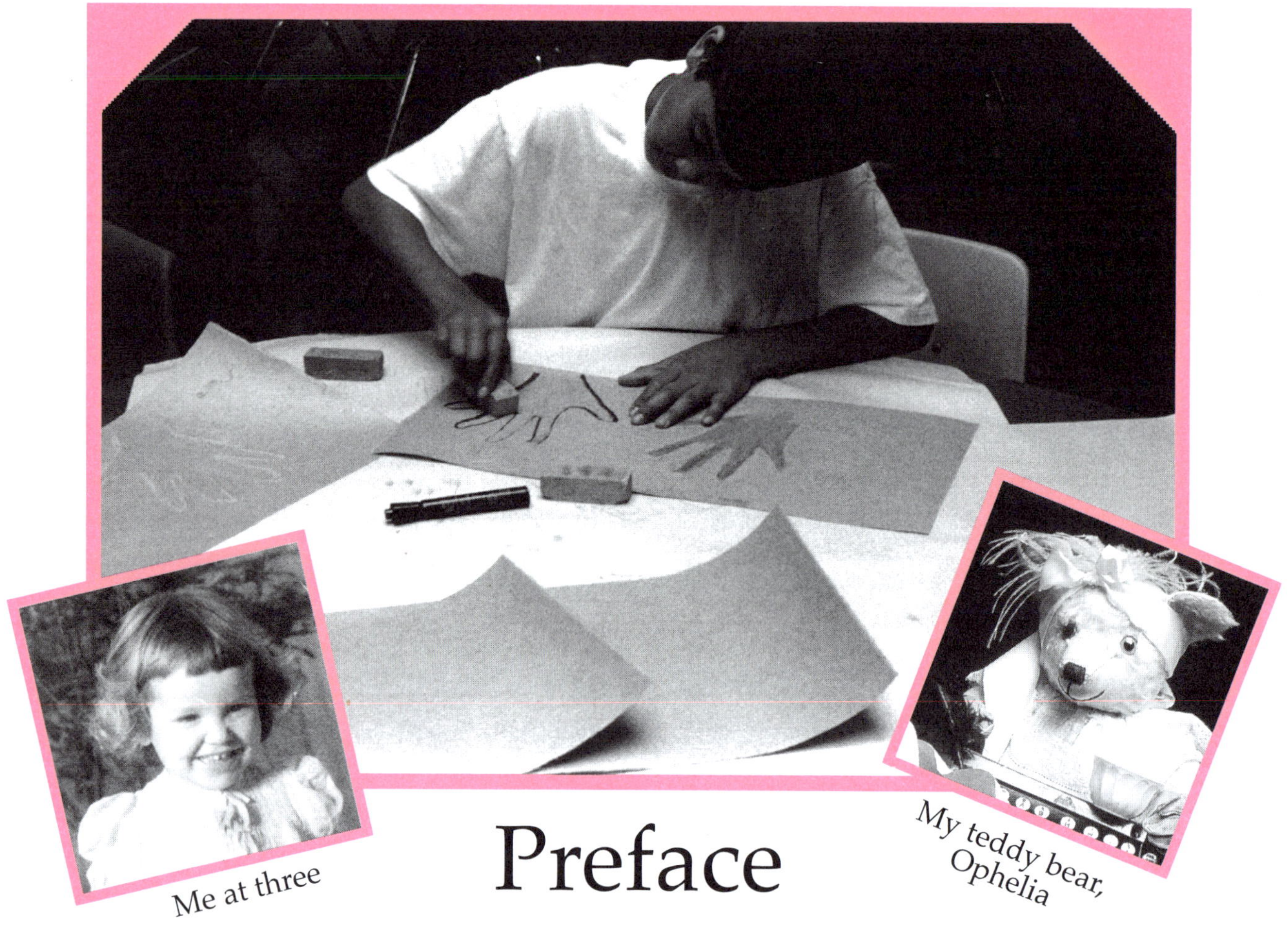

Me at three

My teddy bear, Ophelia

Preface

When I was a child, there was never a thought or a fear on my part or my parents' that I would be confronted with gun violence. It simply didn't exist as it does today. Due to my growing dismay at all the news stories of children hurt or killed by guns, in 1992 I began seriously thinking about a book on the subject, and searched for the voice needed to tell the story.

As the author and creator of books about a teddy bear named Ophelia and a book of manners, *No Bad Bears,* I have taken my bears to quite a few schools at the request of teachers. While at one school, on a lovely June day, I visited grades K-6 with bears Ricky and Sophie and discussed books and manners for forty-five minutes with the children in each class.

There were lively conversations about manners, bears, books, and ideas for books. As the students and I became more comfortable with each other, and with Ricky and Sophie mingling with the kids, I decided to bring up the subject of violence to see if the children were aware of or concerned by the topic.

I was shocked and saddened by the responses to my question. As I gazed out at those beautiful and vivacious faces I heard the truth of violence being told by children. Each child had something important to say. They either personally had encountered a gun or knew someone who had. They knew people—relatives, friends, other children—who had been shot. They knew a student who had committed suicide. They had seen guns on the street and some knew where they could get one. Remember, this was an elementary school.

After one fourth grade class the teacher came up to me and said, "This is the age—this is where we can make the difference in children's perception of violence. I encourage you to follow through with your book idea. Please, for their sake!"

Realizing that communicating directly with children would be vital to the creation of this book, I looked for an opportunity to work with a group of them. It seemed to me that perhaps slightly older children would be appealing role models for younger readers.

I am fortunate to know David Okimoto, director of Atlantic Street Center. Established in 1910 by the deaconesses of the Methodist Church, this was Seattle's first settlement house. ASC has several programs specifically for youth and takes a hands-on approach. I described my project to the staff and they suggested that I work with their Summer Academy program. It just so happened that they had a place for me on Wednesdays with a group of thirty middle-school-age kids.

Taking a roll of brown wrapping paper, a box of colored chalk, the two teddy bears, and a bag of See's lollipops, I blithely entered the halls of the Summer Academy. After an energetic "orientation" the first day, we began the serious work. Discussions about the causes and consequences of violence were followed by sessions of drawing and more discussions.

I wanted the group to create a poster, and had already arranged for Stephen Pannone at Tim Girvin Design to help me pull the kids' efforts into a finished project.

Marsha Burns, a photographer and my good friend, documented our work and helped achieve my dream: a book and accompanying poster (the cover) that tell a fictional story about the truth of what can happen when a child has a gun. Marsha was extremely generous in allowing me to use her photographs as I saw fit. The kids thought she was great and loved to have their pictures taken. The strength and vitality of the kids pictured here could never have been captured by models or drawings. These are real kids at play and at work.

I began to call my merry band of pranksters the "Live and Direct Kids" from Atlantic Street, and gave this name to the foundation that will receive the proceeds from this book.

I am extremely fond of these kids. Their energy and intellect are constant sources of pleasure. We owe them the chance to shape the future and to learn from our mistakes. Without the children we have nothing.

I thank the kids for allowing me to share their summer and, I hope, the coming seasons of their lives. I also thank their parents for allowing me to share their photographs with you, the reader. The story that follows uses photographs of real children (and real teddy bears!) and their real artwork to illustrate a fictional look at what violence is doing to our young people and what they, in turn, can do about it.

These wonderful kids, as well as all the children you know, are the future. The future is now.

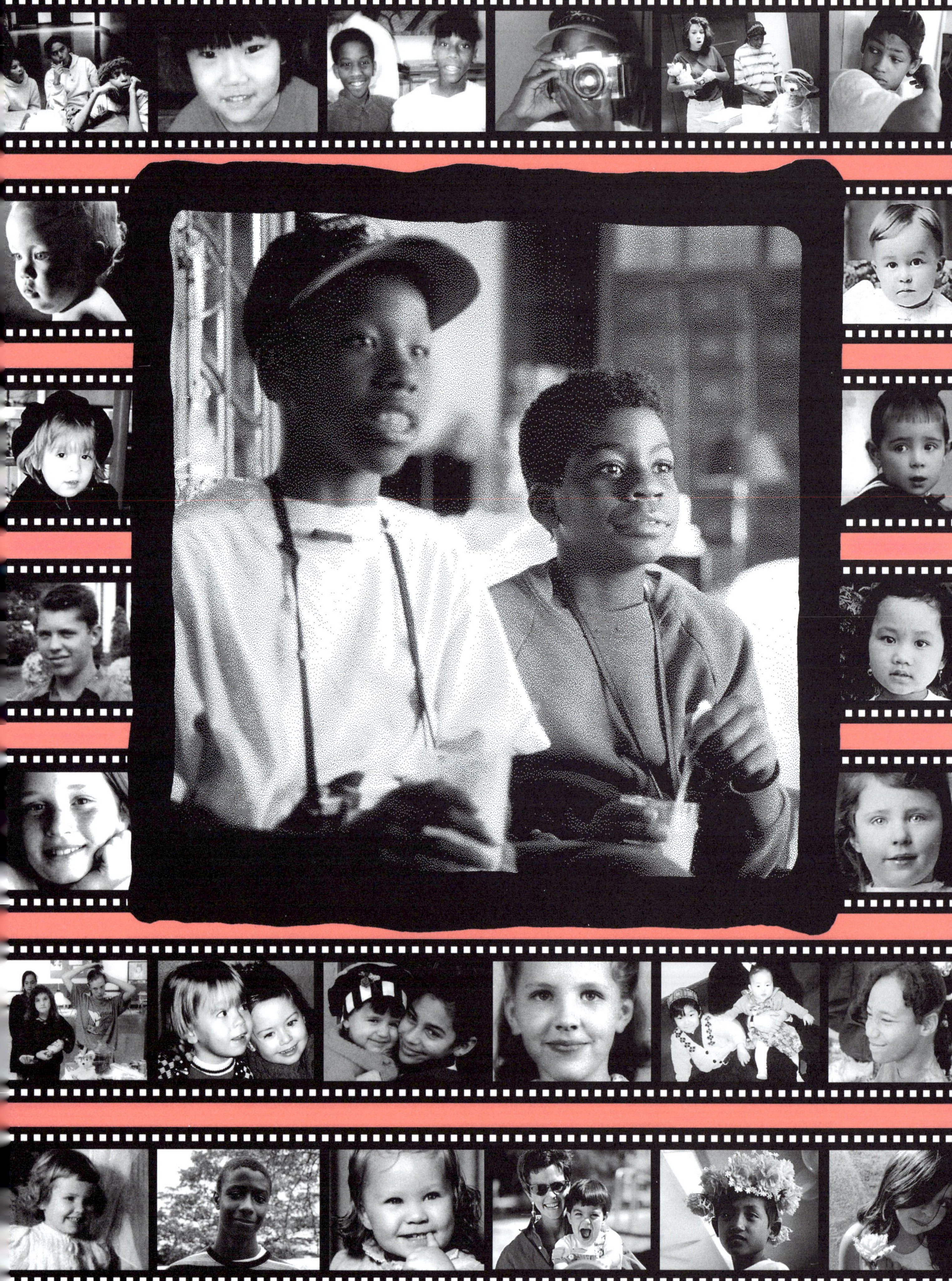

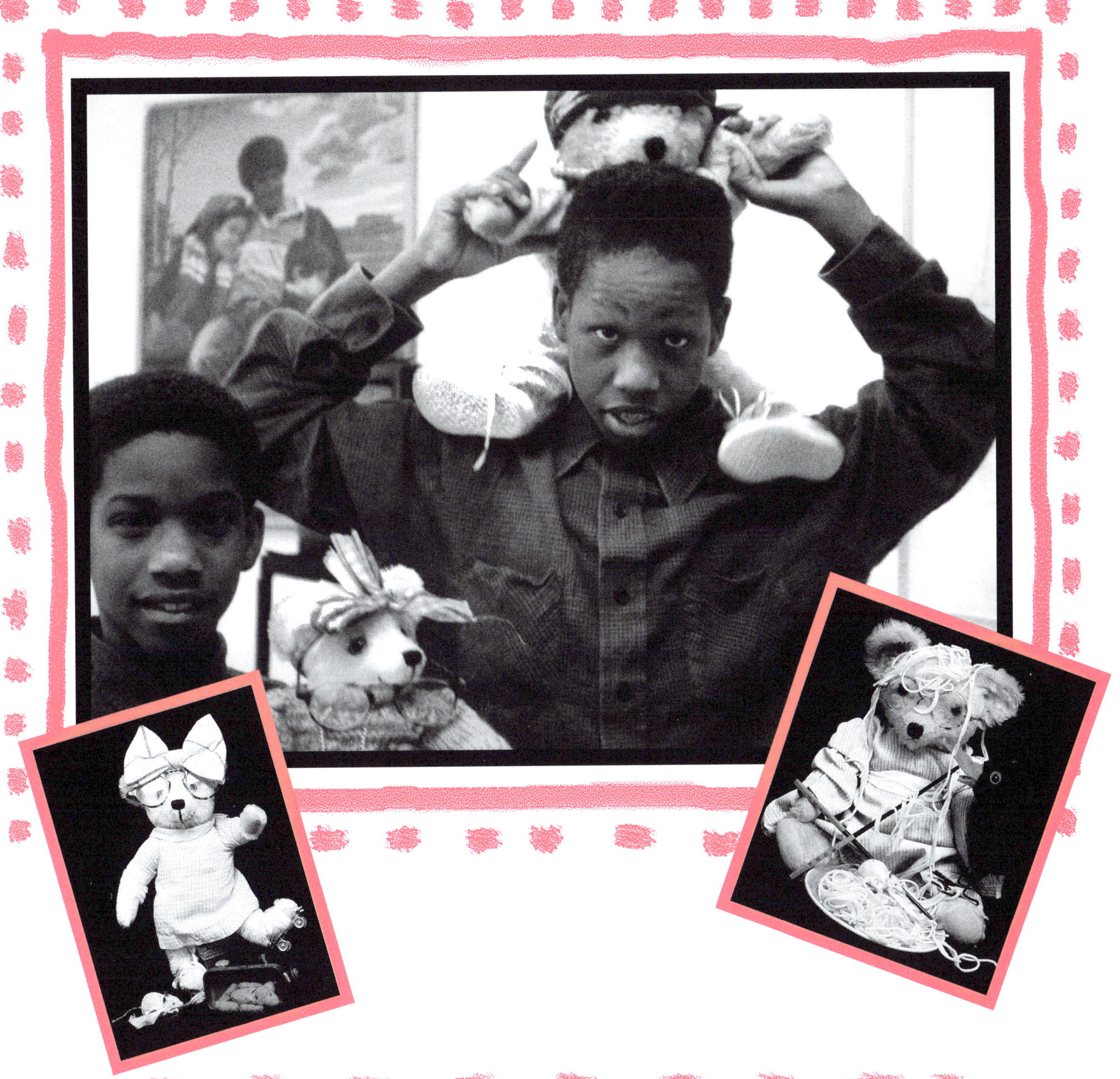

Not Like the Movies

Starring Ricky and Sophie

A Story for Kids

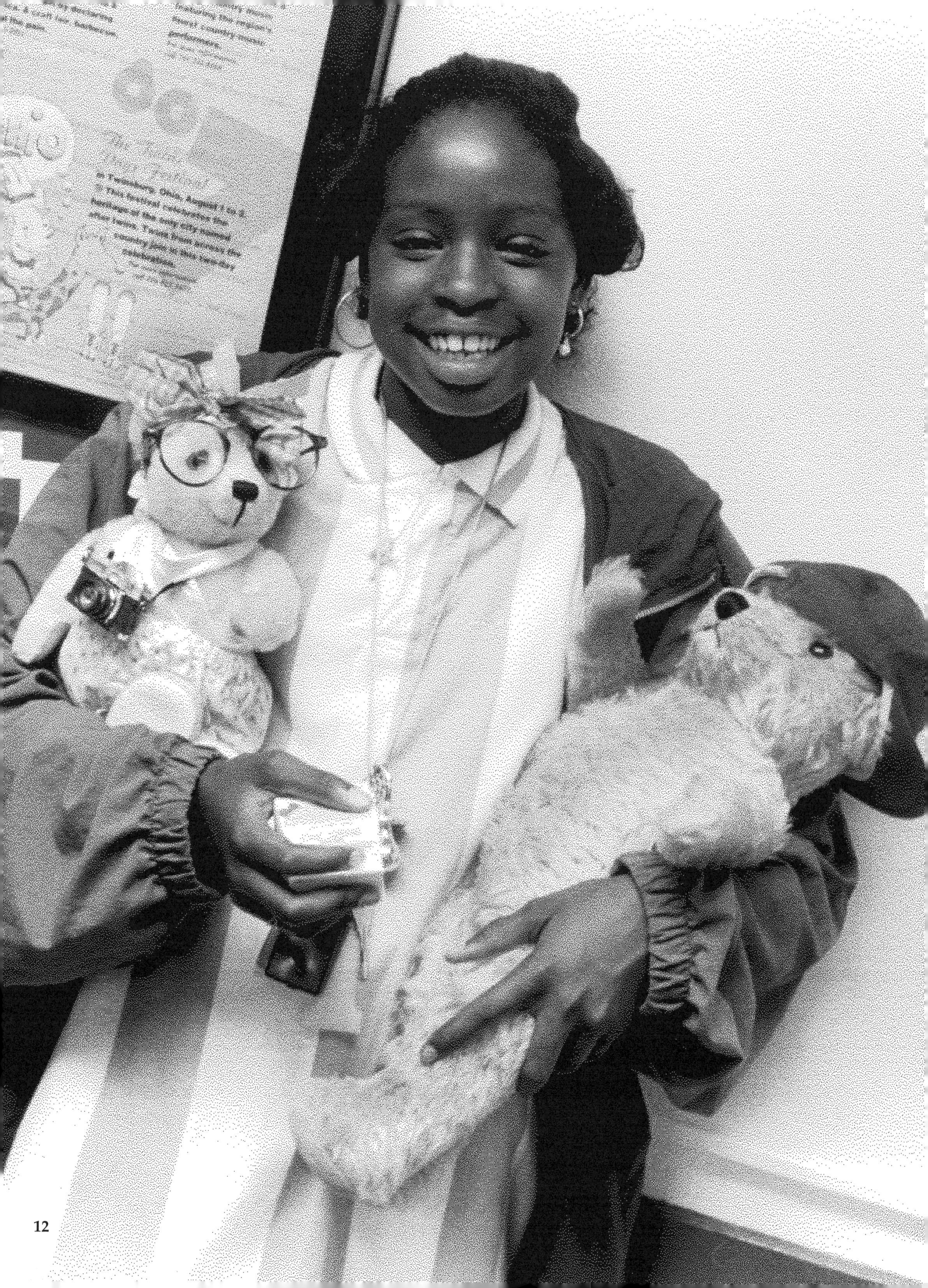

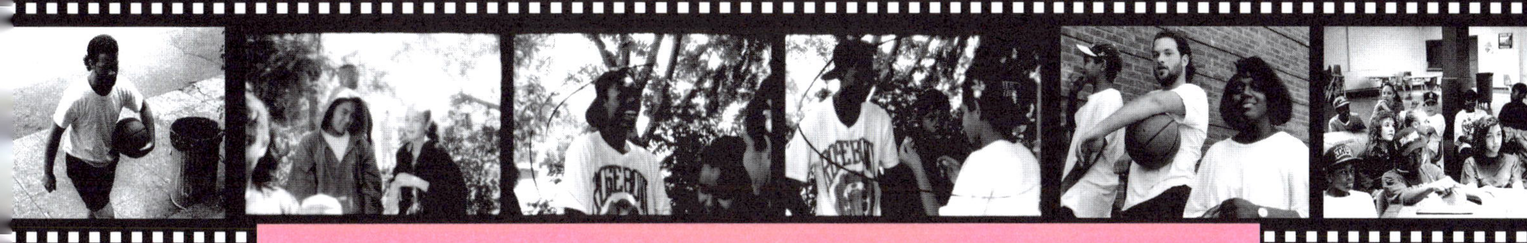

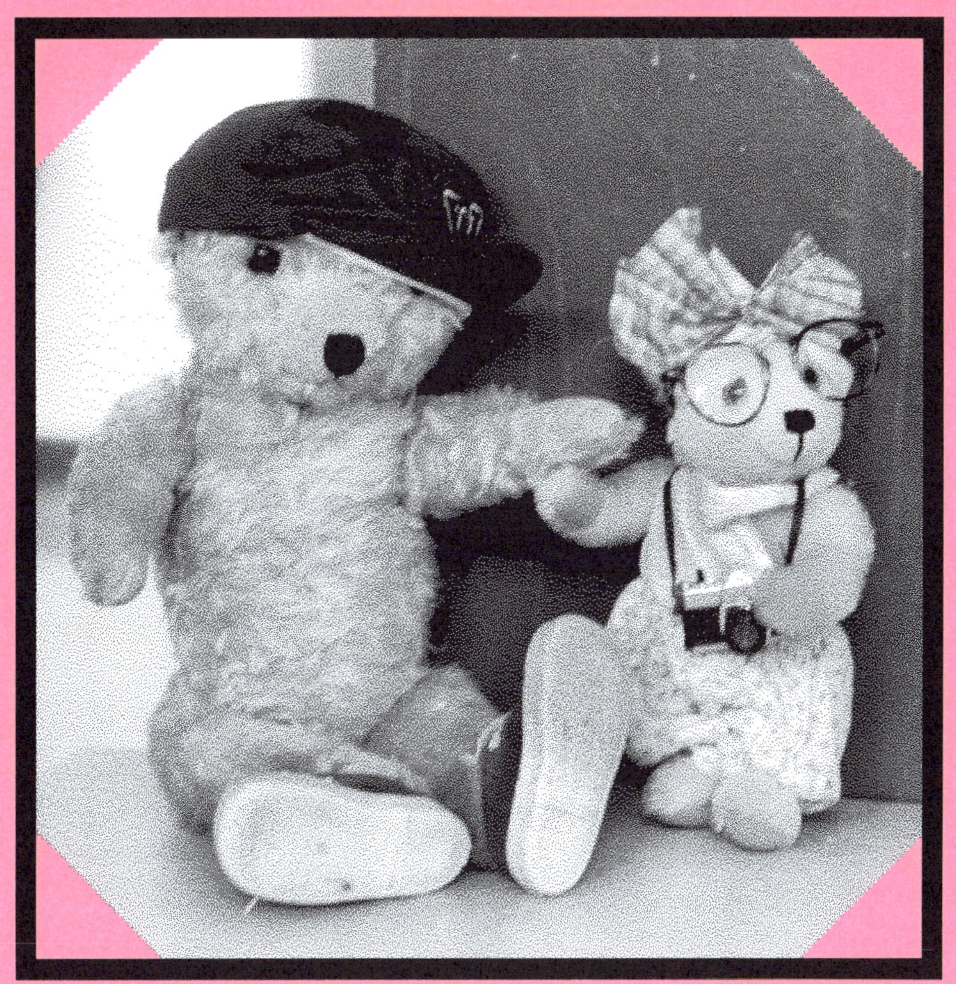

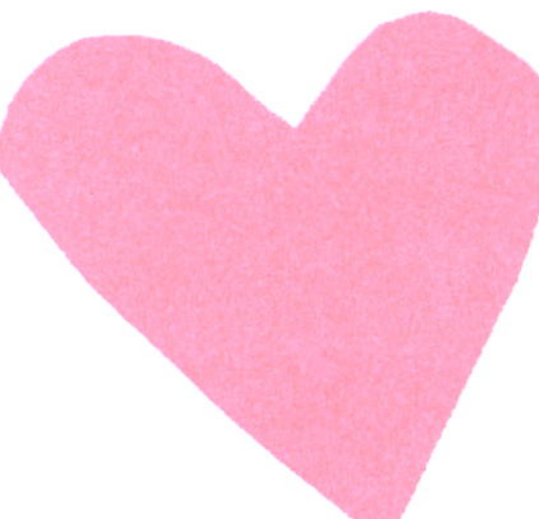

Ricky and Sophie loved to go to school.

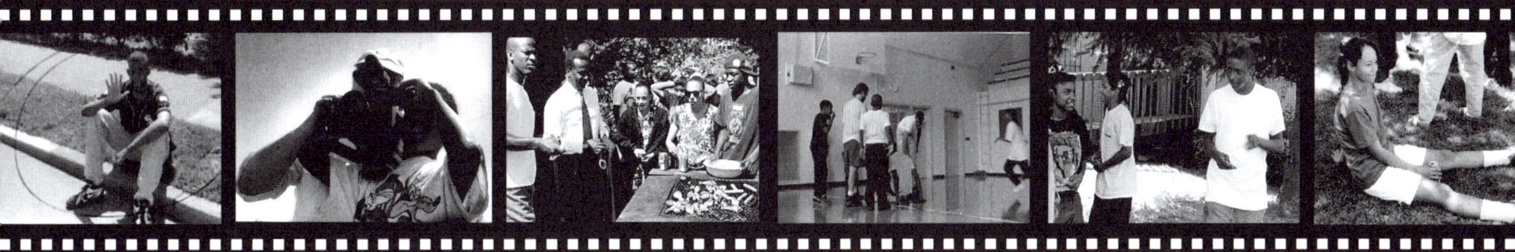

There was always something interesting to learn.

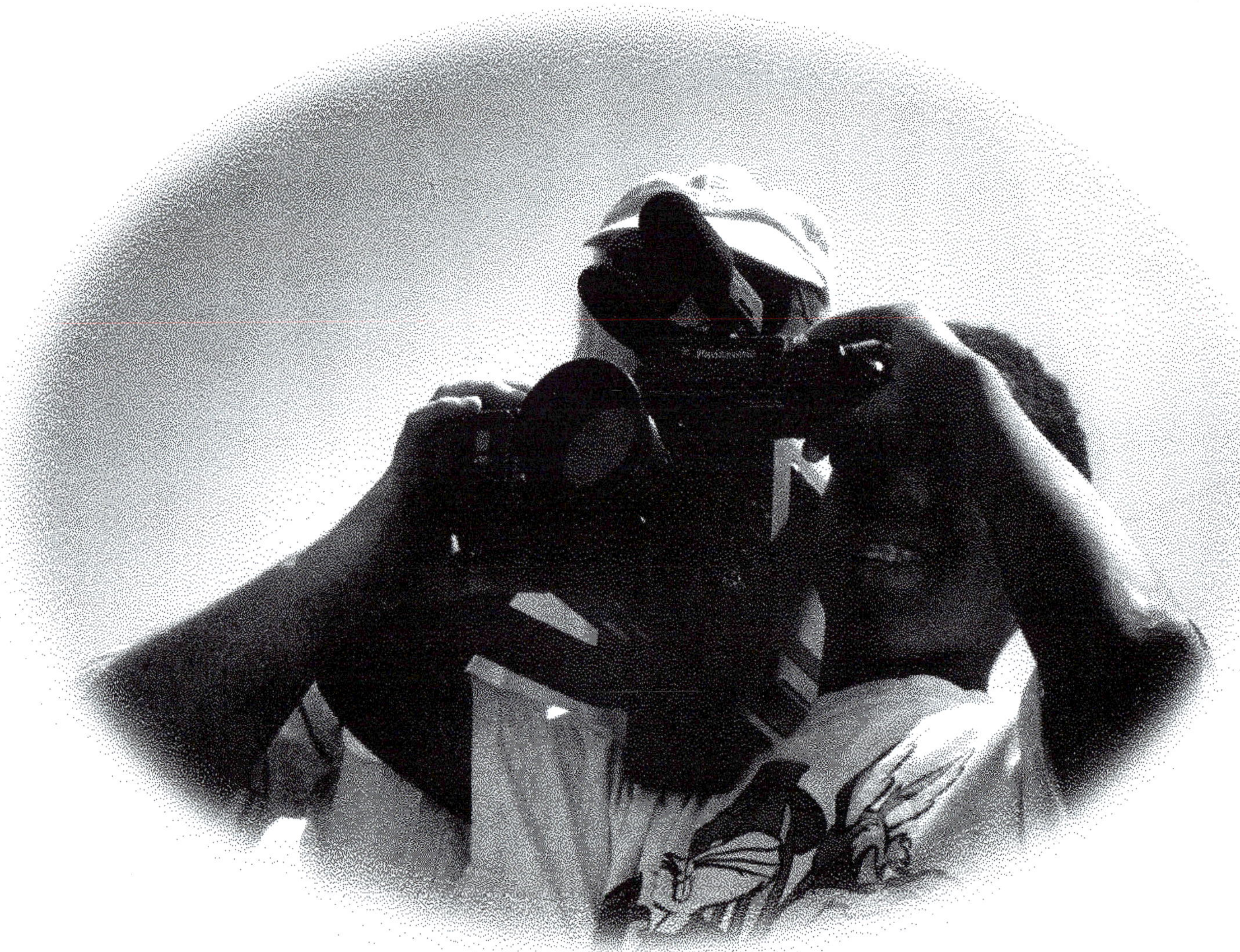

But even more important, there were lots of kids to play with.

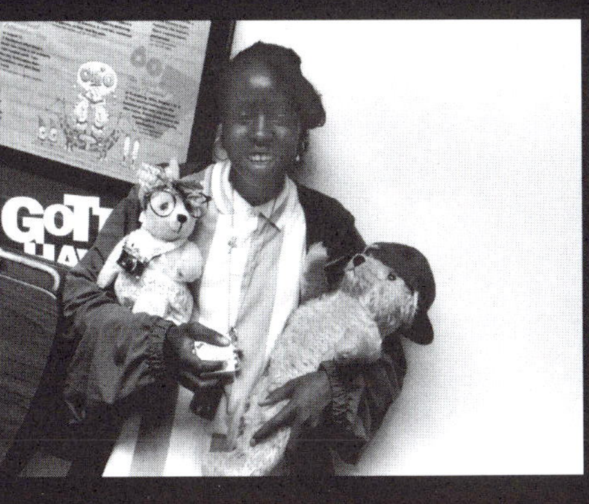

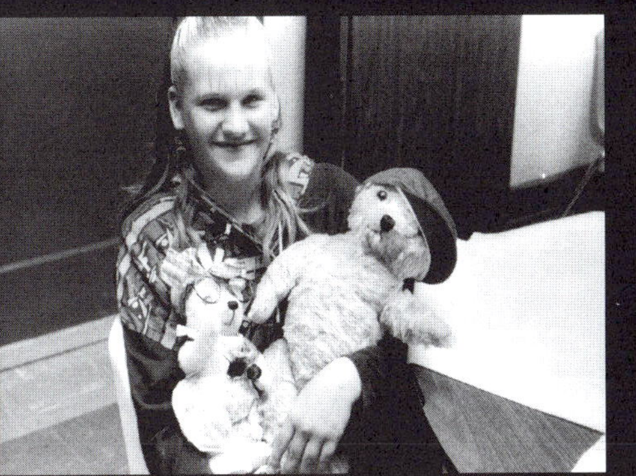

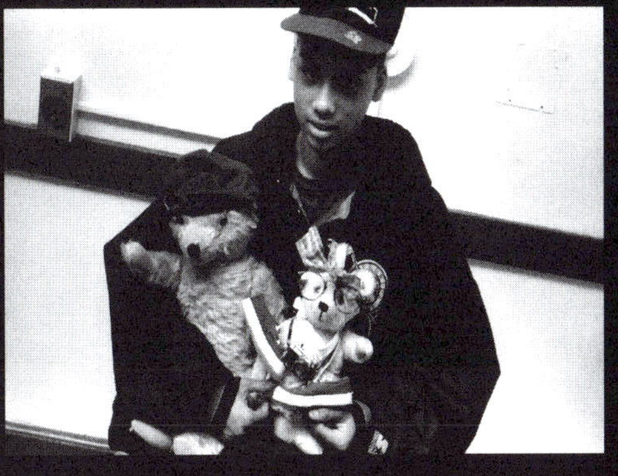

The bears loved the kids.

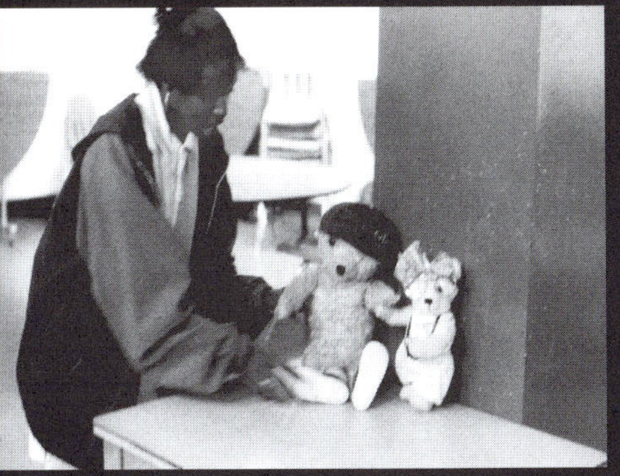

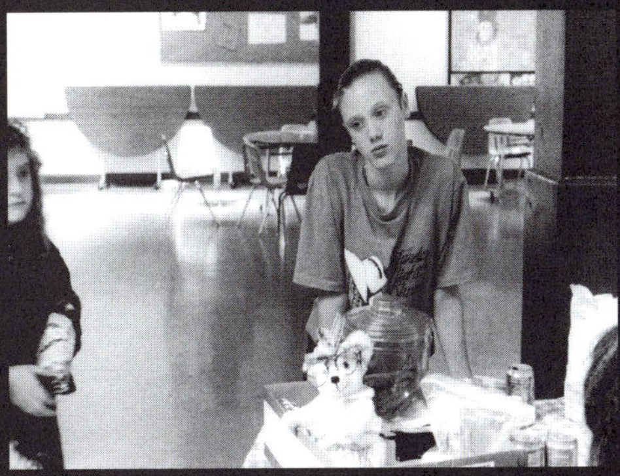

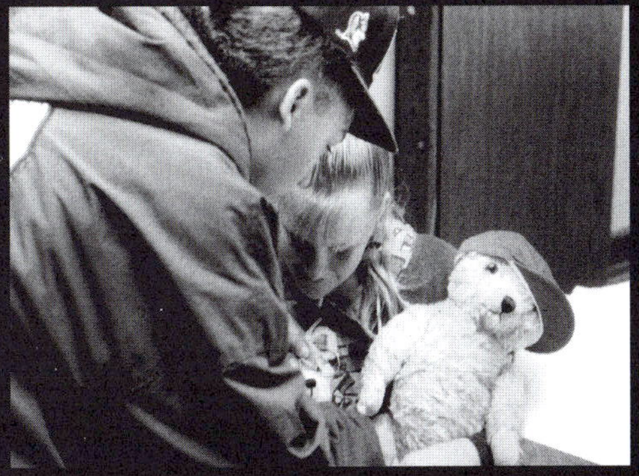

They loved the girls,

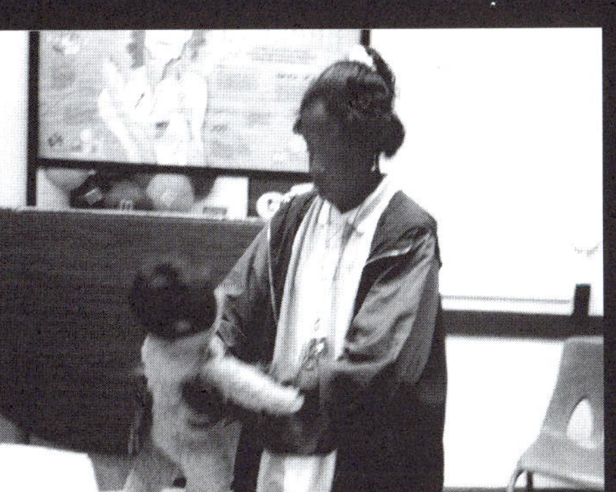

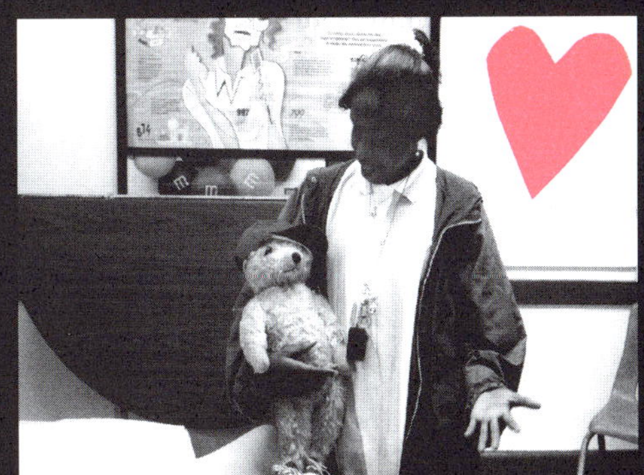

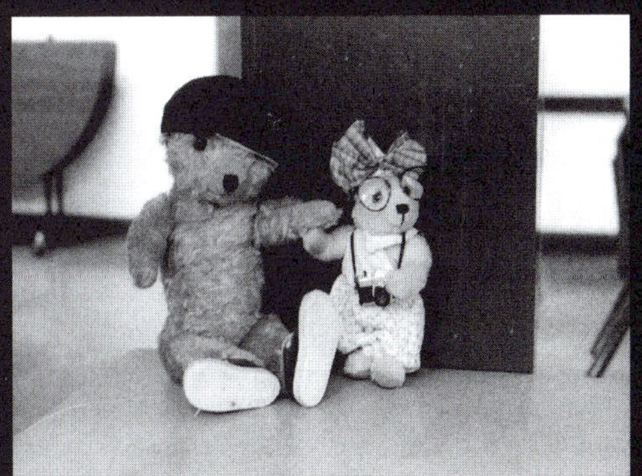

they loved the boys.

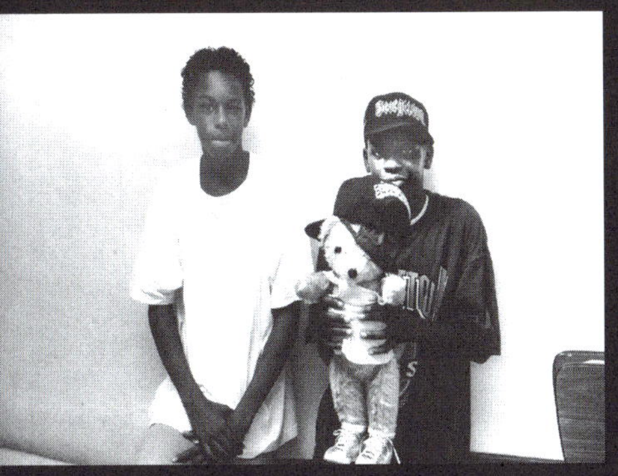

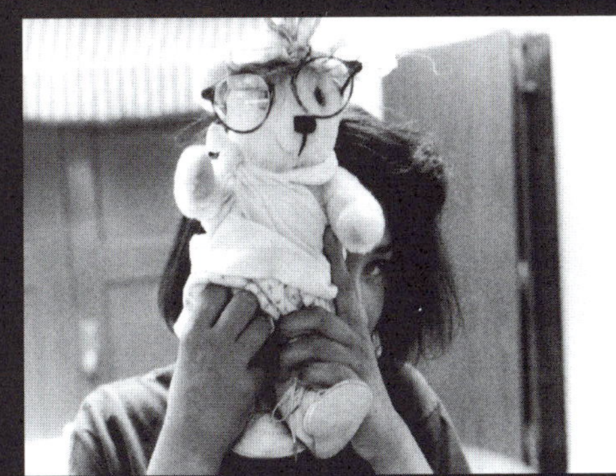

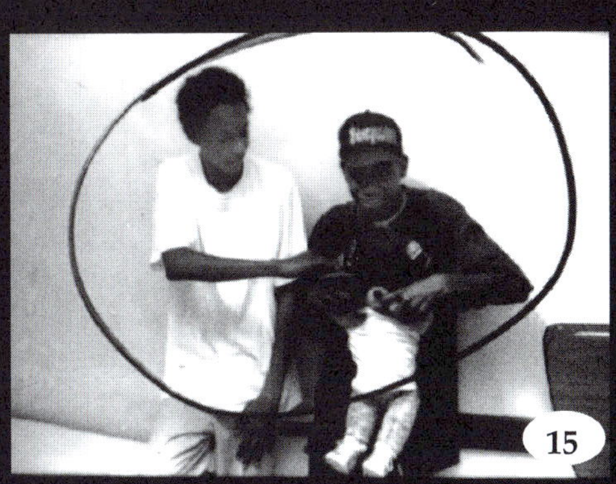

Renée-La'kisha-Mamie-Nico
n-Angelina-Raschel-Natash
Halina-Shandi-Tonika-Vale
sha-Morgana-Naomi-Yolan
hie-Lupe-Christina-Wi
Lyne
-An
a
t

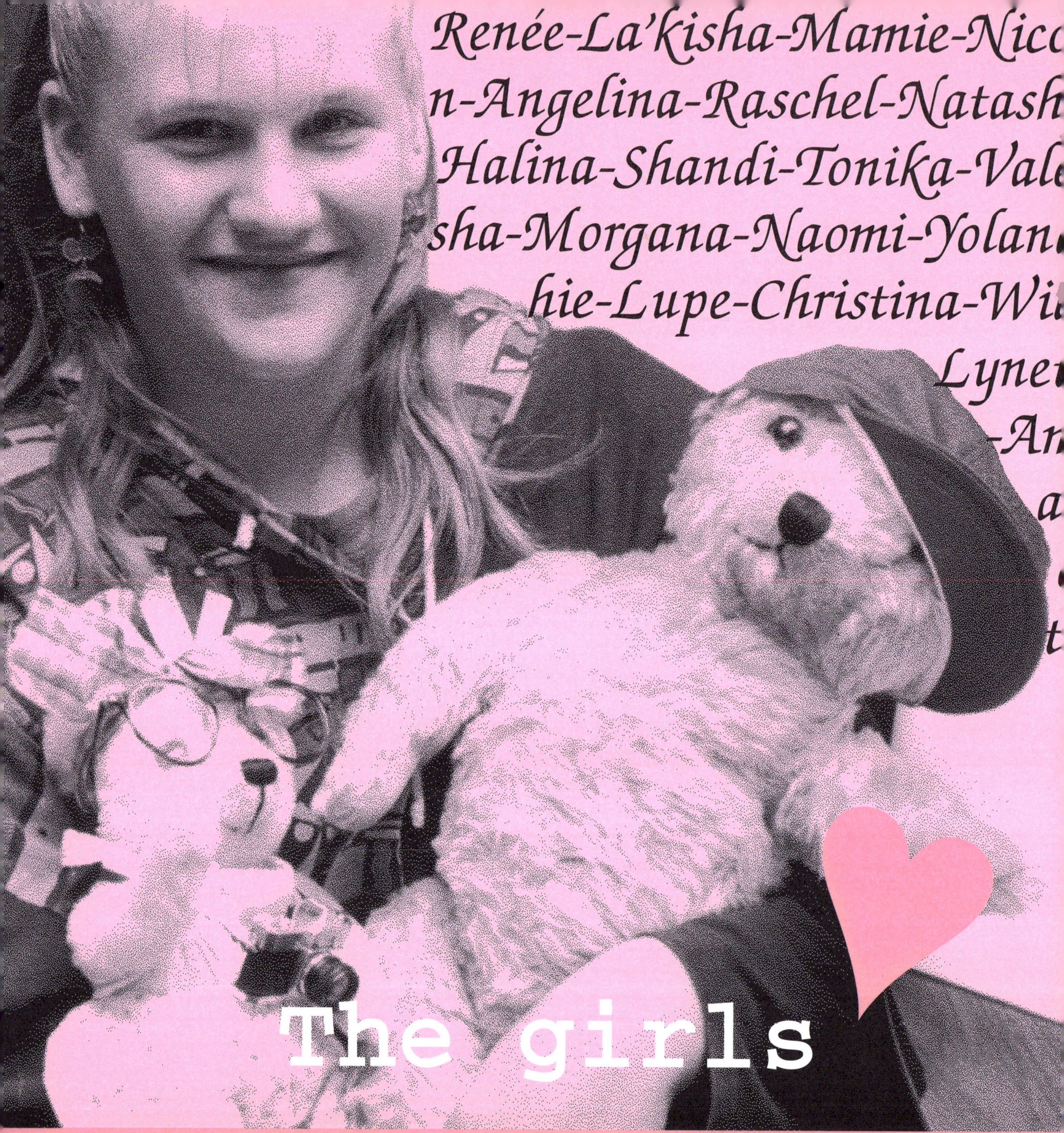

The girls

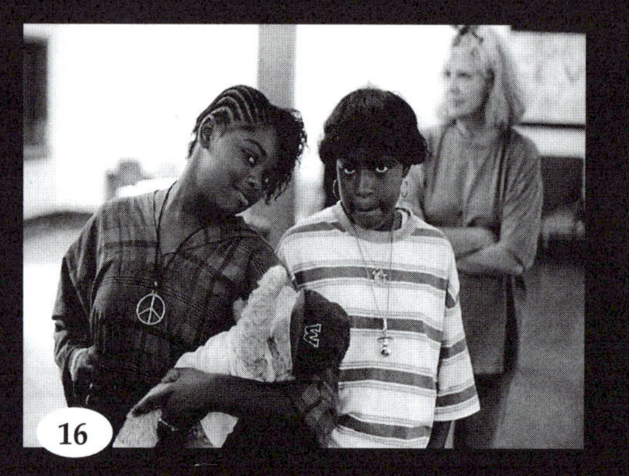

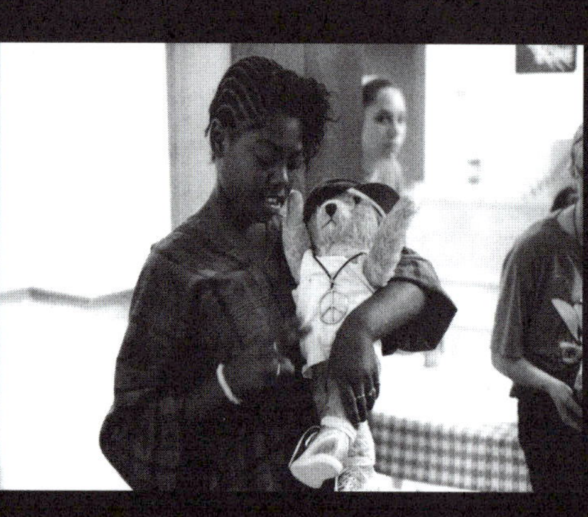

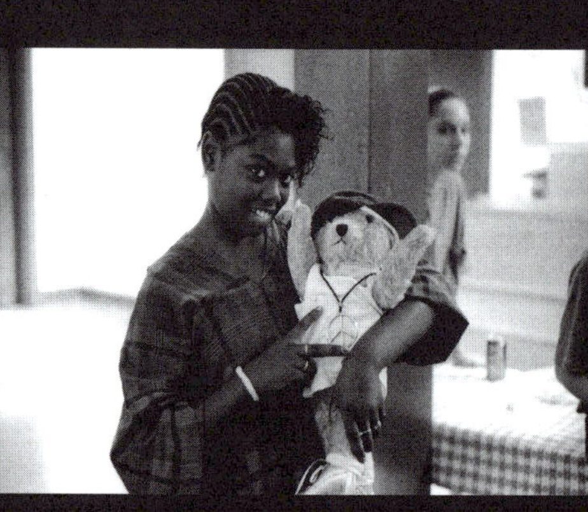

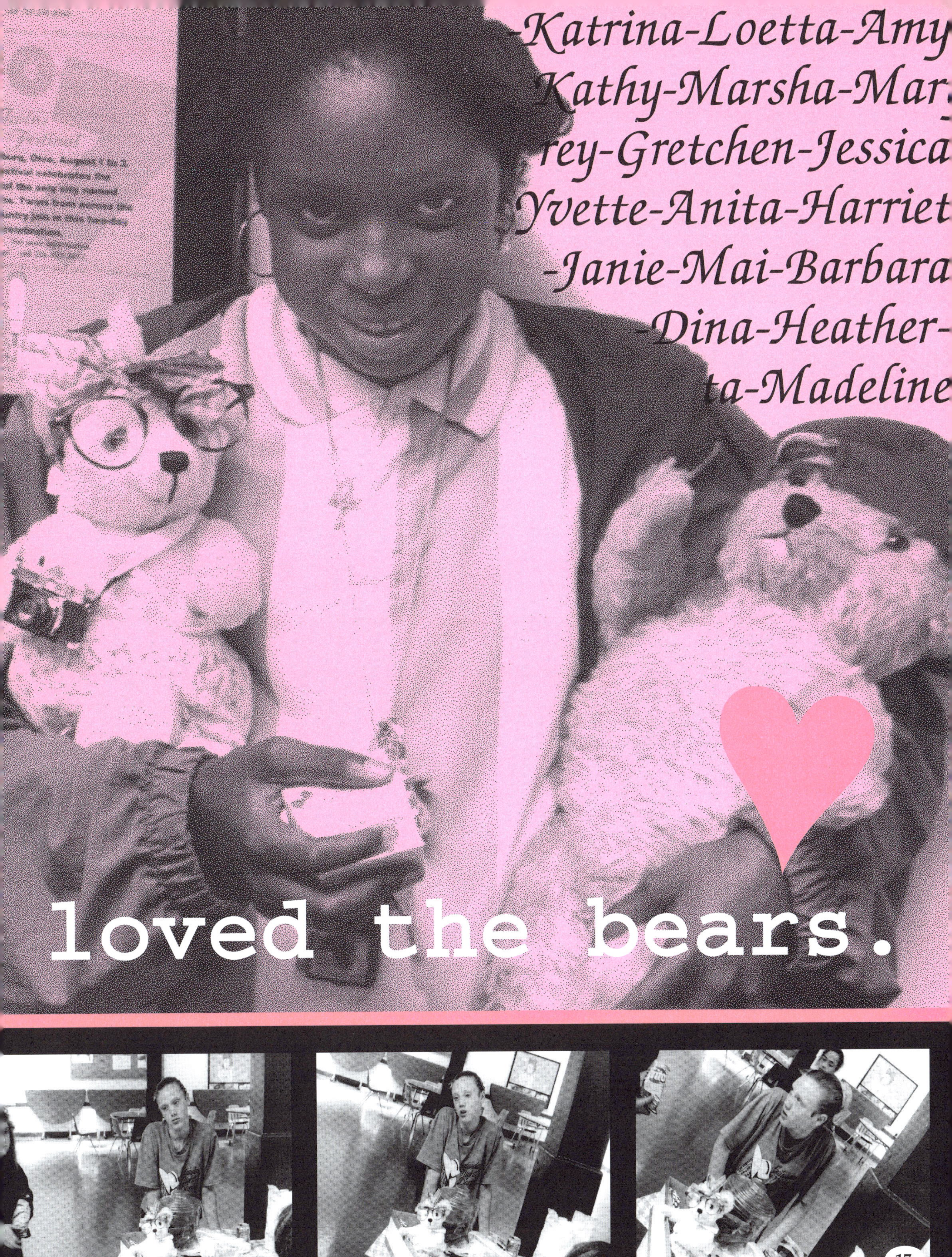
-Katrina-Loetta-Amy
Kathy-Marsha-Mar
rey-Gretchen-Jessica
Yvette-Anita-Harriet
-Janie-Mai-Barbara
-Dina-Heather-
ta-Madeline
loved the bears.

Gabe-Henry-Troy-Mark-Marvin-Daryl-Kenneth

Avery-Nick-Steven-David-Andrew-Elmer-Brandon-Willie

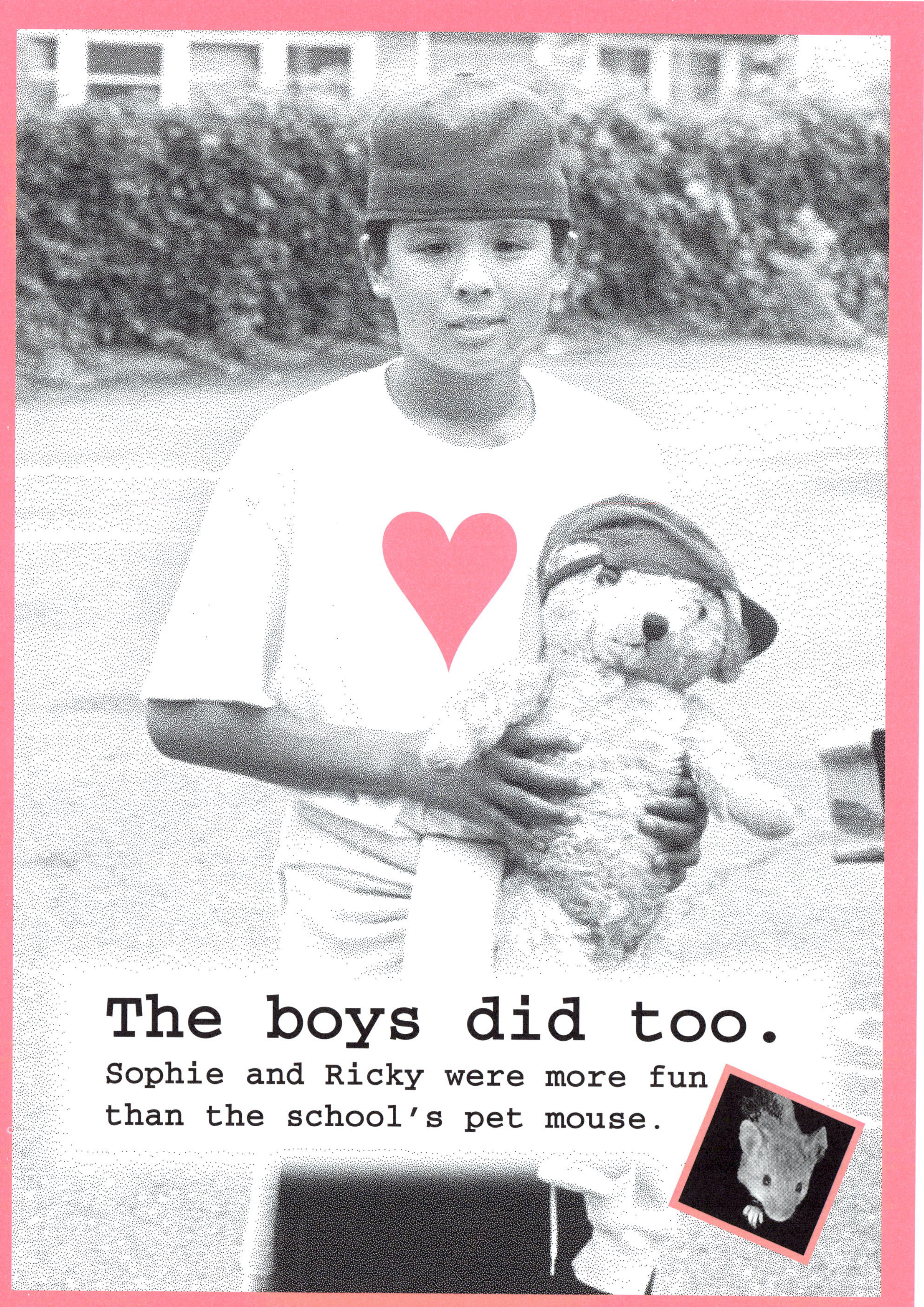

Jeremy-Eddie-Chauncey-TuCun-Randy-Alan

Paul-Antoine-Dion-Jesse-Angel-Carlos-Marc-Fia-Ricky

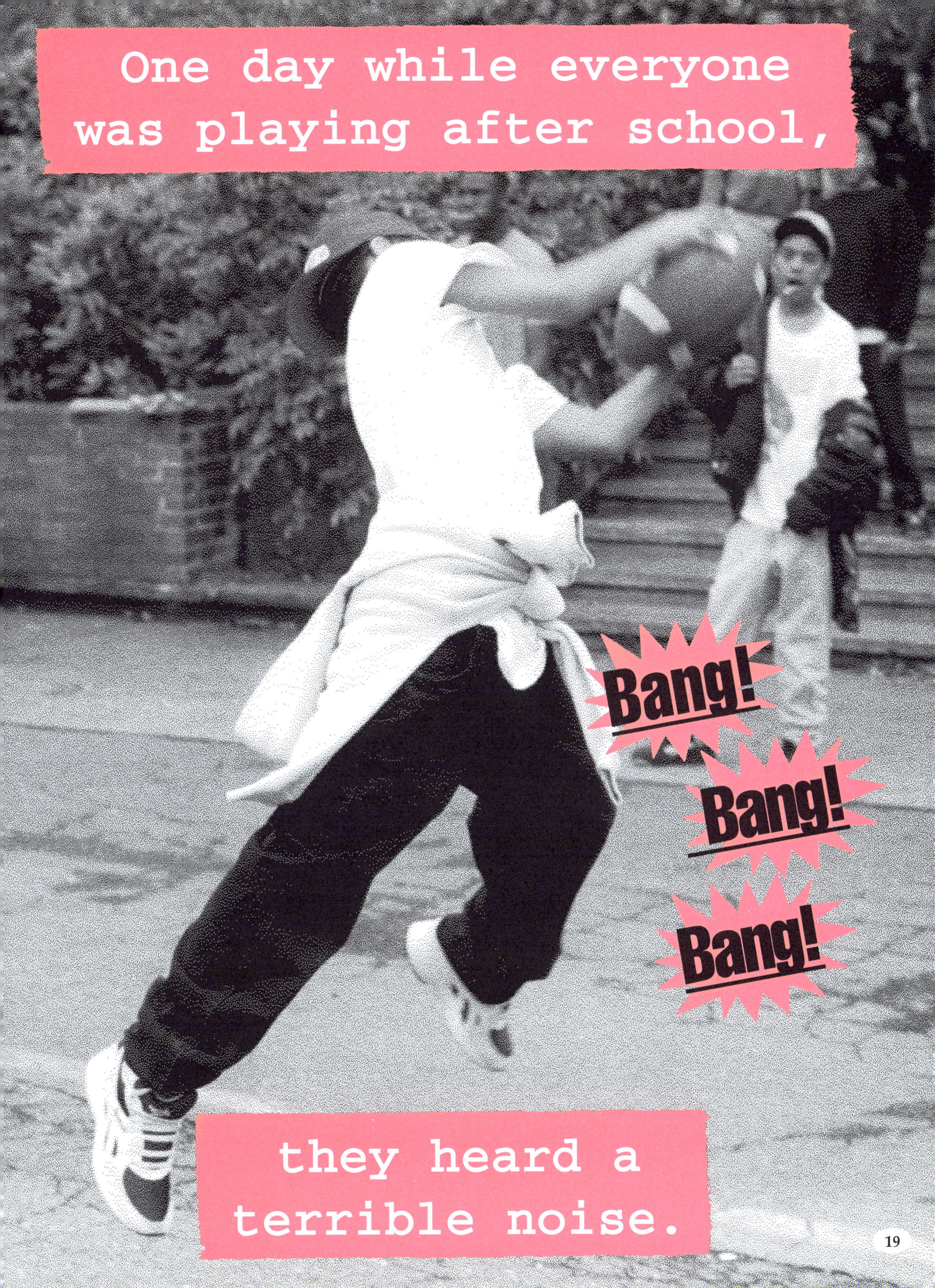
One day while everyone was playing after school,
Bang!
Bang!
Bang!
they heard a terrible noise.

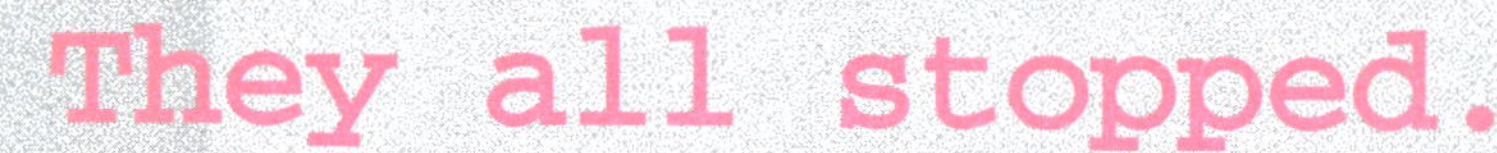

They all stopped.

"That sounded like a gun," said the tall girl. "Is everyone here?"

"Everyone but Florida and her brother Tony," Ricky answered.

"I'm worried," cried Sophie. "Lets call a police officer."

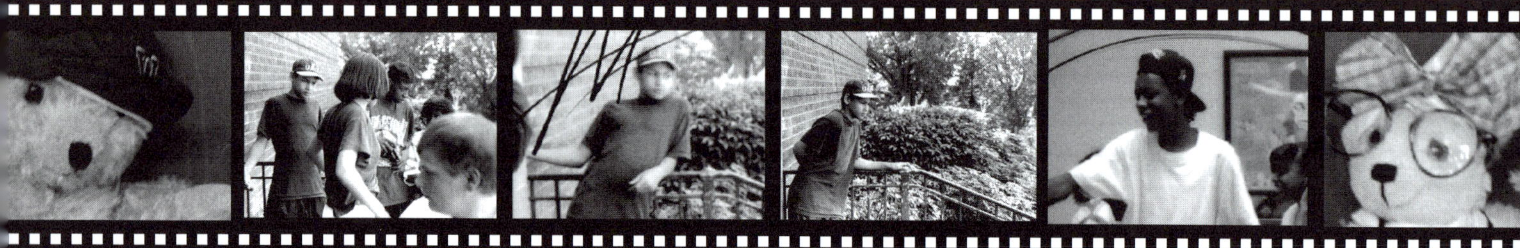

When the officer arrived, he asked, "Did you hear gunshots? What else did you hear or see?"

"We heard sirens," Ricky answered.

"That was the aid car. Someone must be hurt," said the officer.

The kids and the bears didn't know what to do.

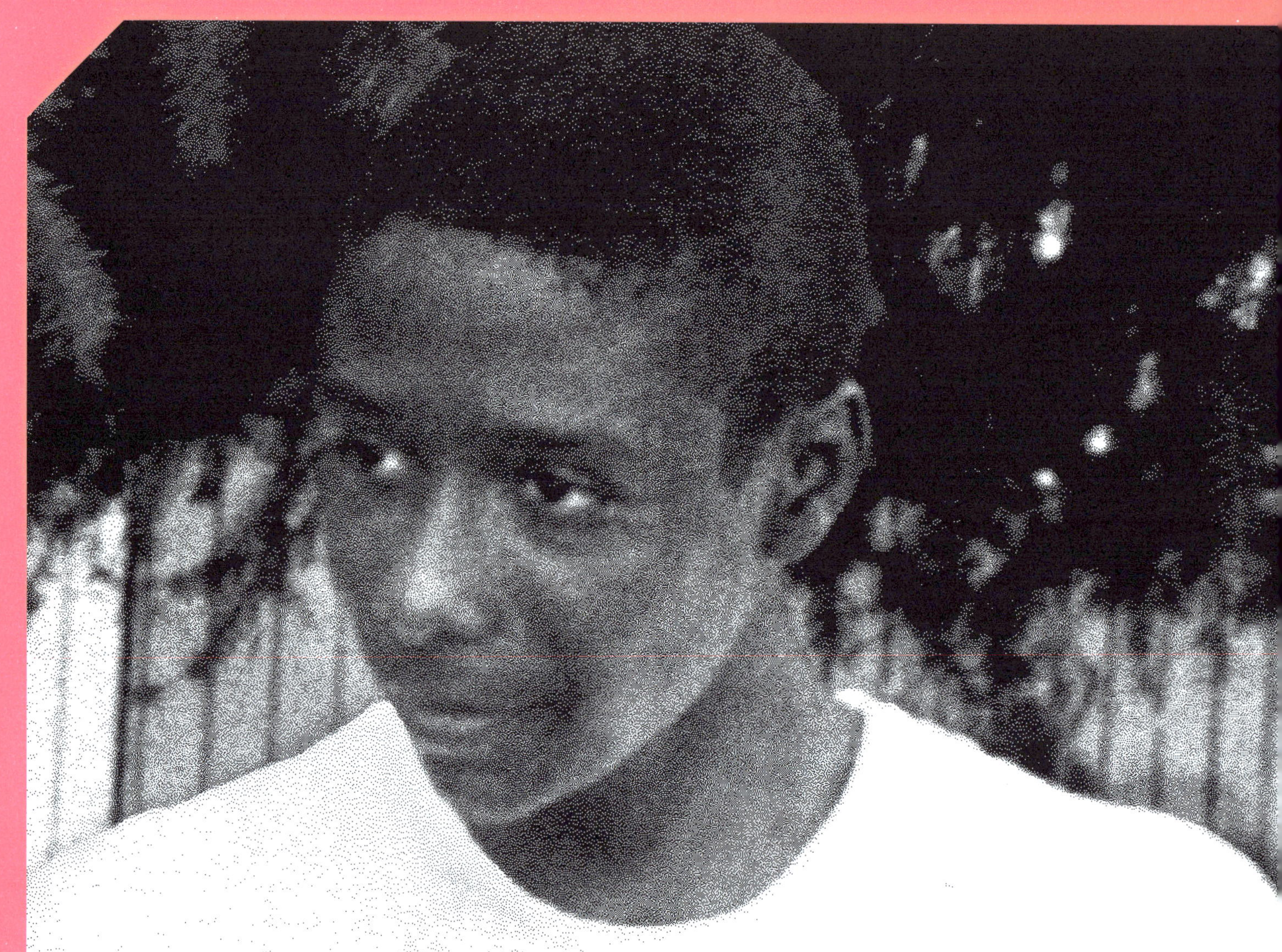

Ricky ran and asked the tall boy if he had seen Florida and Tony. "No," he answered. "I saw the aid car and police cars. As a matter of fact, I saw two aid cars." Ricky felt all sweaty and his stomach began to hurt. He told the tall boy he was very worried. The tall boy tried to comfort Ricky.

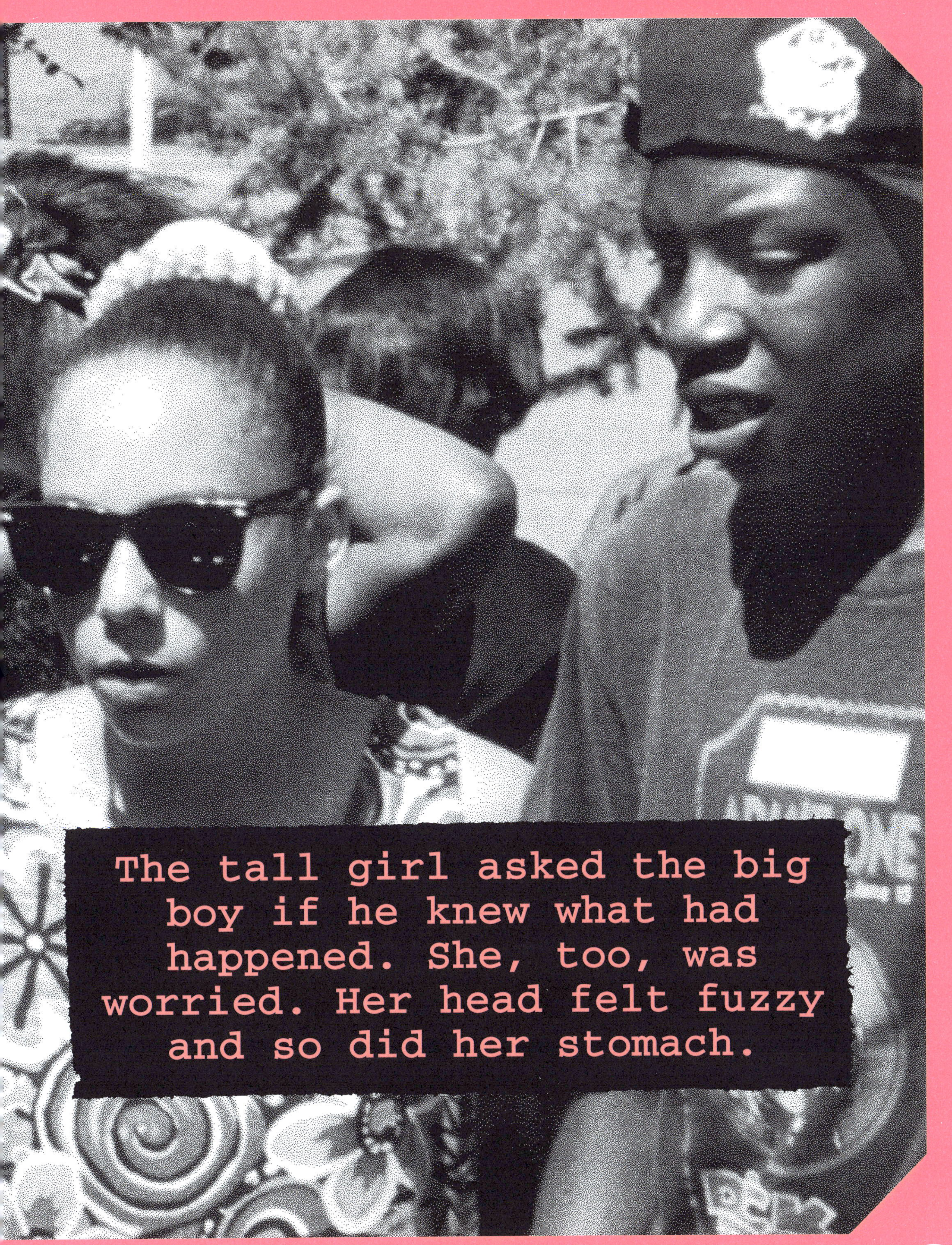

The tall girl asked the big boy if he knew what had happened. She, too, was worried. Her head felt fuzzy and so did her stomach.

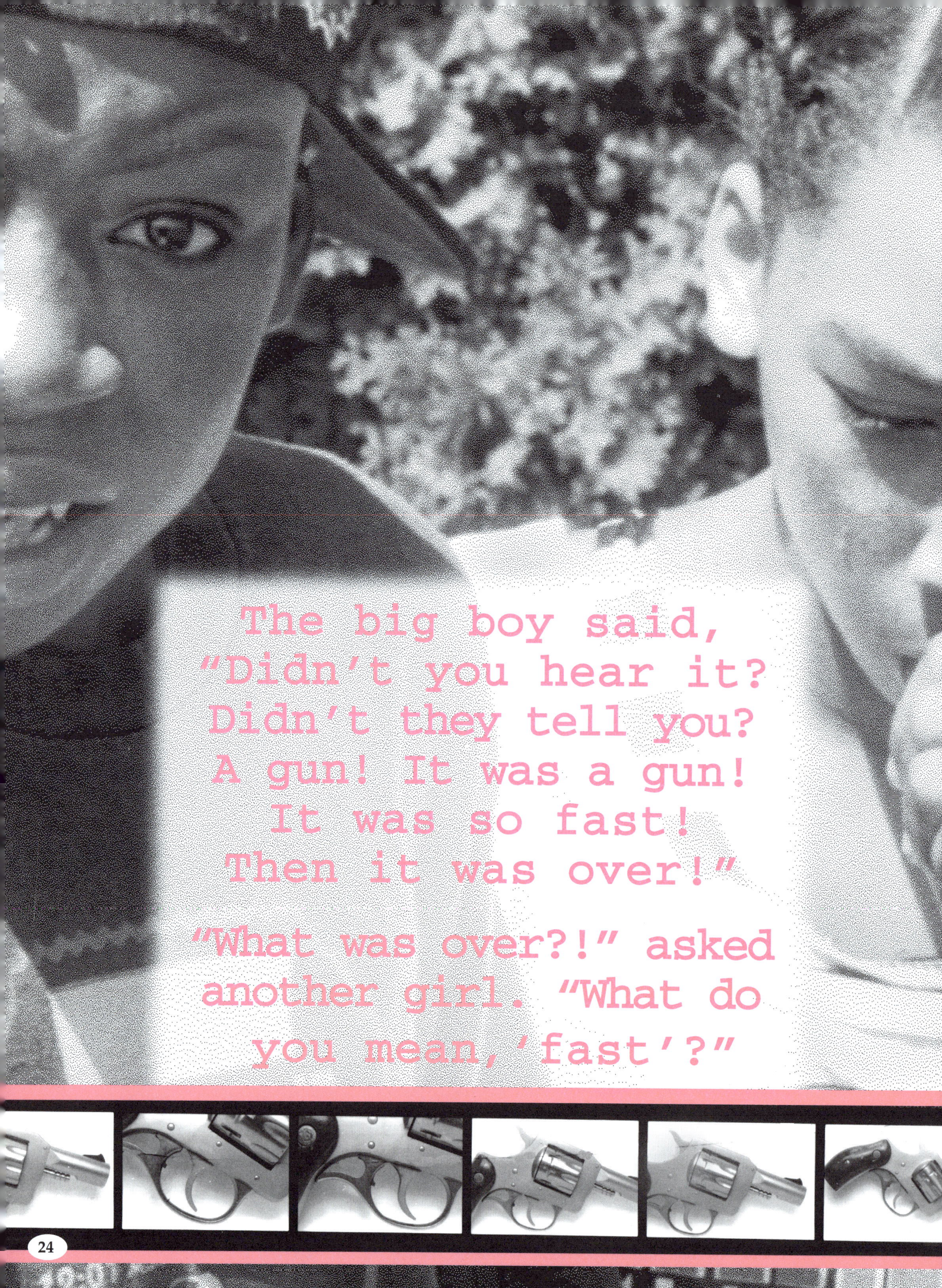

The big boy said,
"Didn't you hear it?
Didn't they tell you?
A gun! It was a gun!
It was so fast!
Then it was over!"

"What was over?!" asked
another girl. "What do
you mean, 'fast'?"

"What did the gun do?" asked Ricky.

"It did what guns always do! They hurt and kill," the big boy answered.

"Who did the gun hurt?" Ricky wanted to know.

The big boy answered, "I'm afraid it was Florida and Tony."

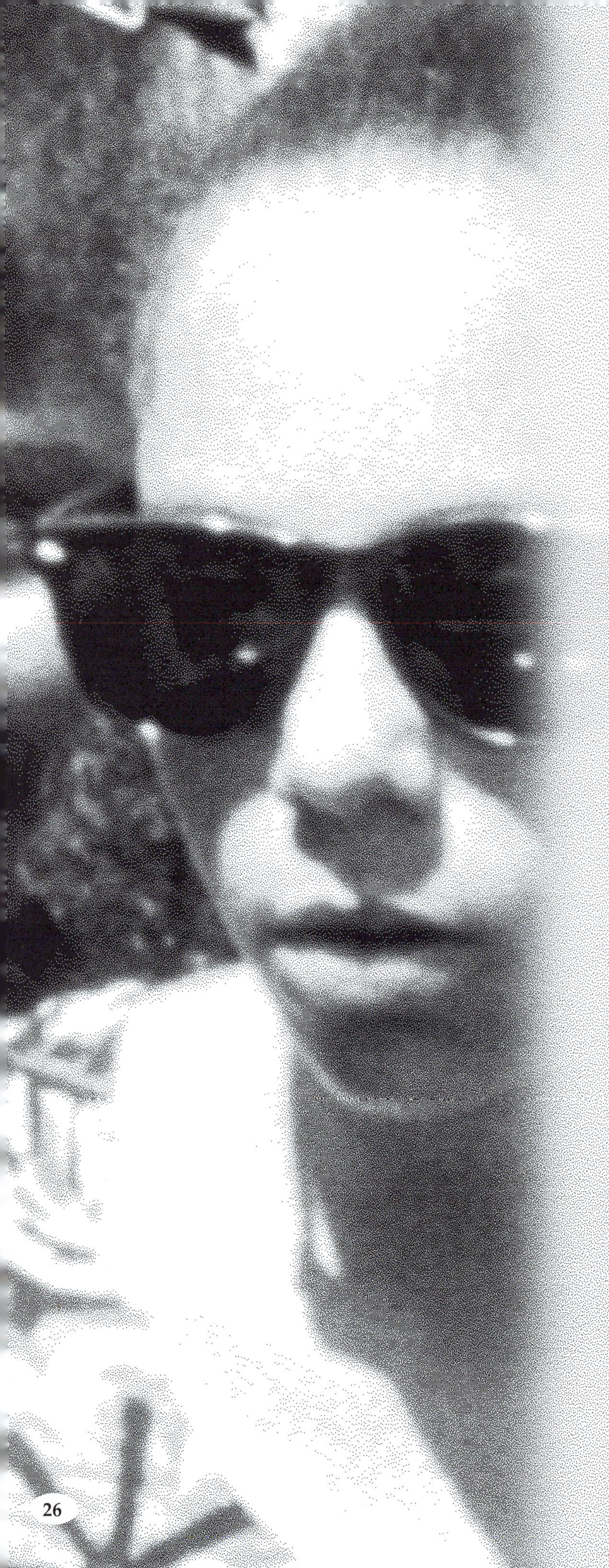

"How do we find out what happened?" cried a little girl.

"The aid cars must have gone to the hospital. I heard a policeman say he was going to the blood bank," answered the tall girl. "We'll go to the emergency room and ask about our friends, but you all must be very quiet and stay close to me."

The kids were filled with fear, and so were the bears.

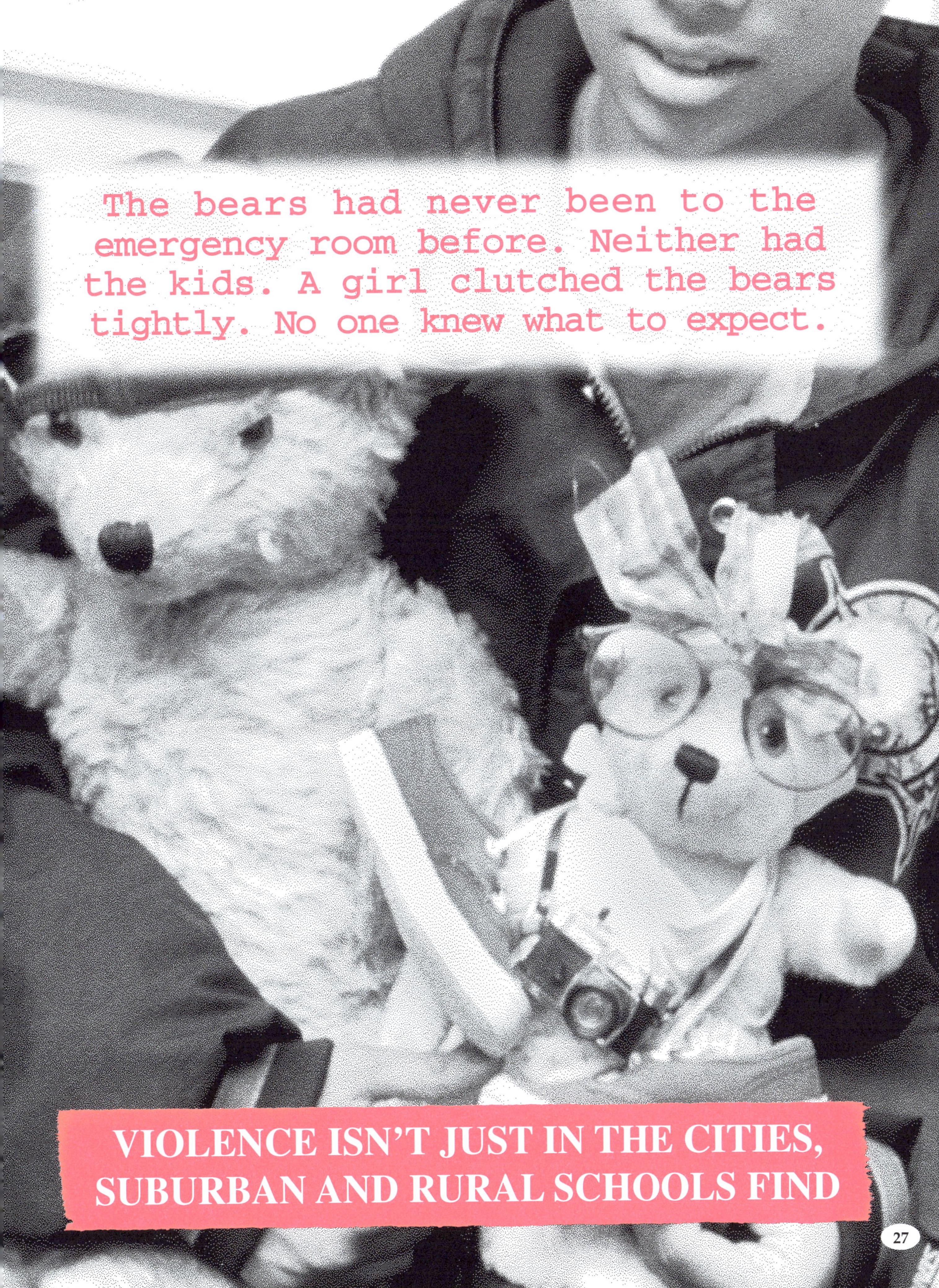

The bears had never been to the emergency room before. Neither had the kids. A girl clutched the bears tightly. No one knew what to expect.

VIOLENCE ISN'T JUST IN THE CITIES, SUBURBAN AND RURAL SCHOOLS FIND

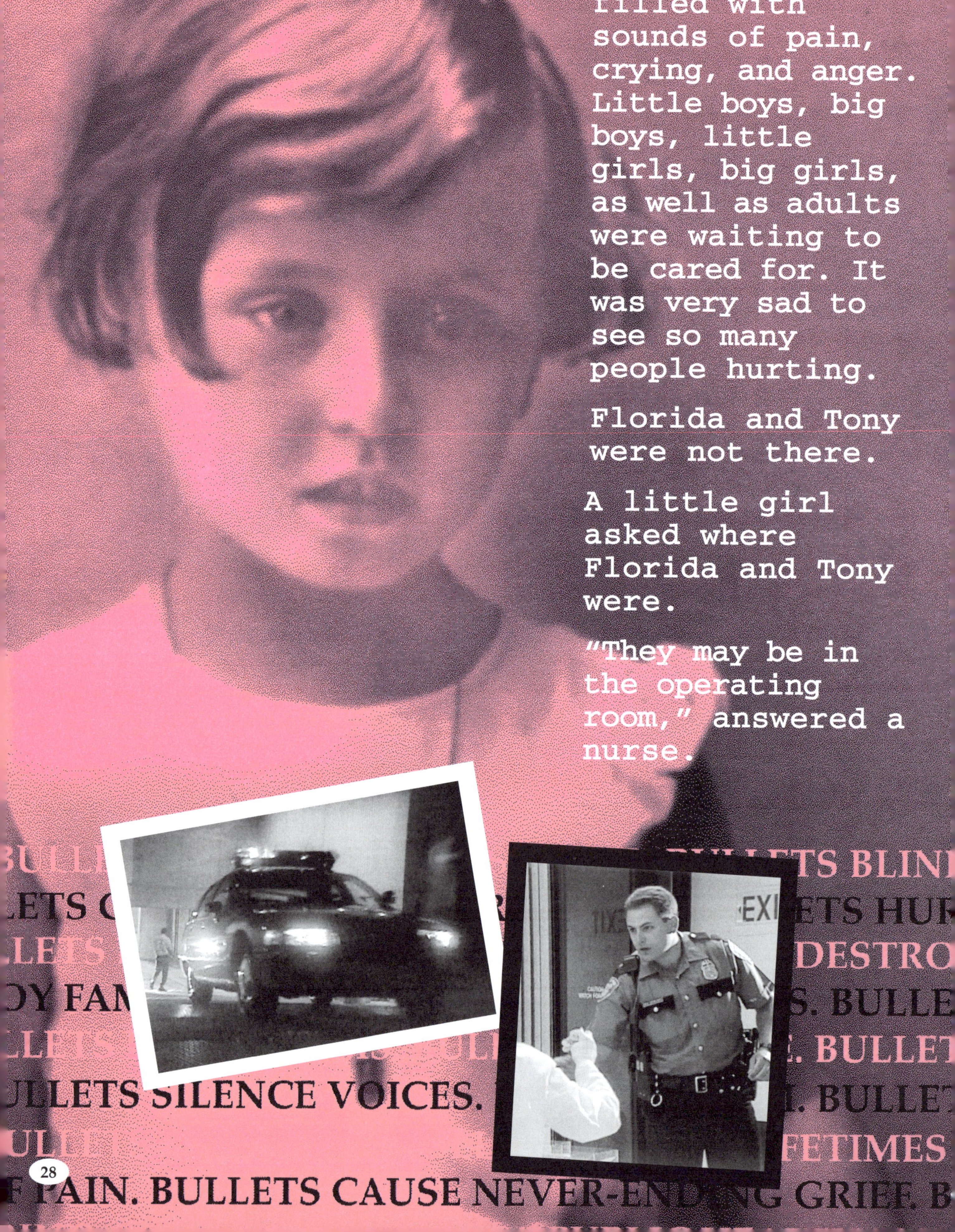

The room was filled with sounds of pain, crying, and anger. Little boys, big boys, little girls, big girls, as well as adults were waiting to be cared for. It was very sad to see so many people hurting.

Florida and Tony were not there.

A little girl asked where Florida and Tony were.

"They may be in the operating room," answered a nurse.

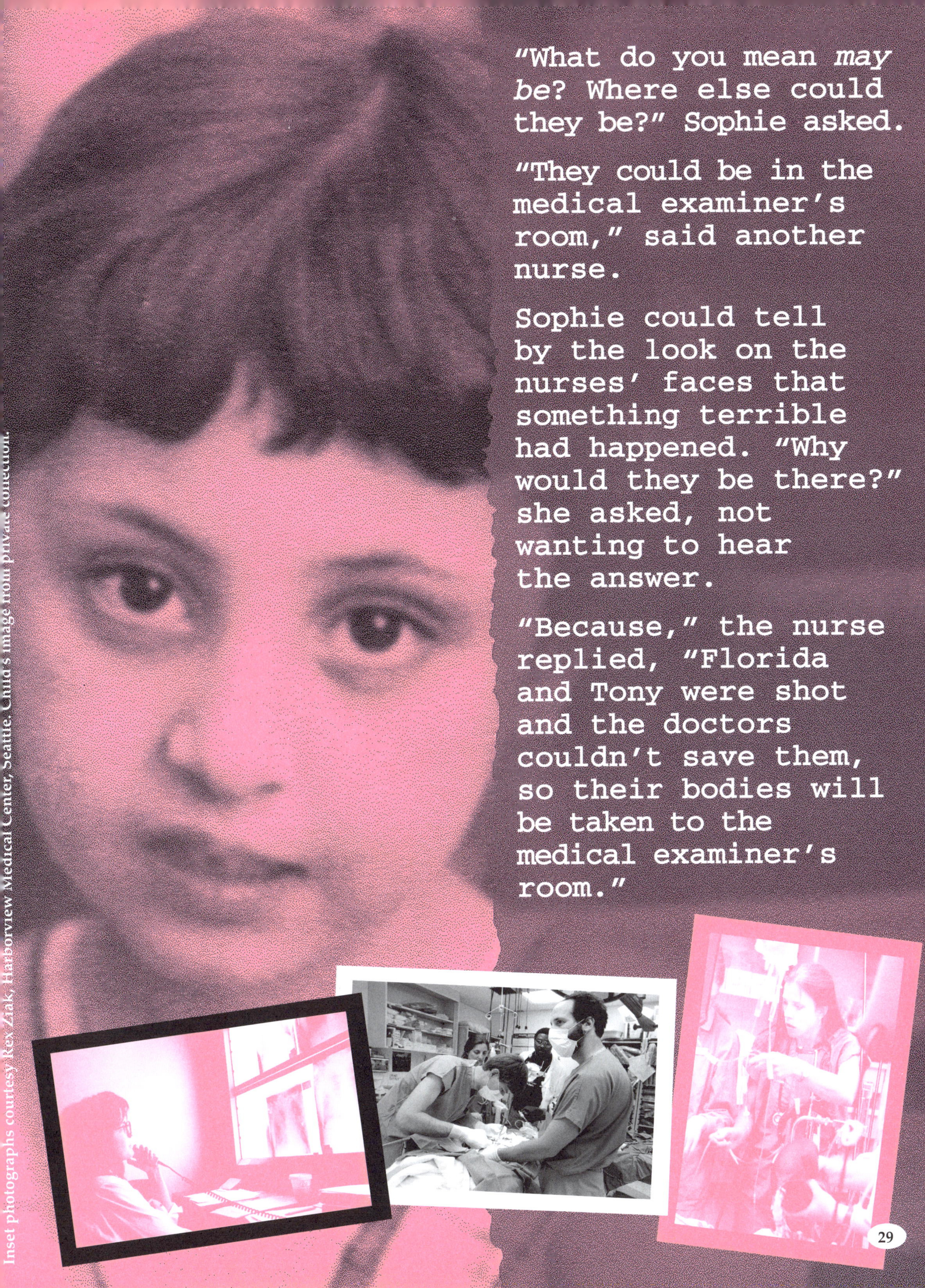

"What do you mean *may be*? Where else could they be?" Sophie asked.

"They could be in the medical examiner's room," said another nurse.

Sophie could tell by the look on the nurses' faces that something terrible had happened. "Why would they be there?" she asked, not wanting to hear the answer.

"Because," the nurse replied, "Florida and Tony were shot and the doctors couldn't save them, so their bodies will be taken to the medical examiner's room."

Inset photographs courtesy Rex Ziak, Harborview Medical Center, Seattle. Child's image from private collection.

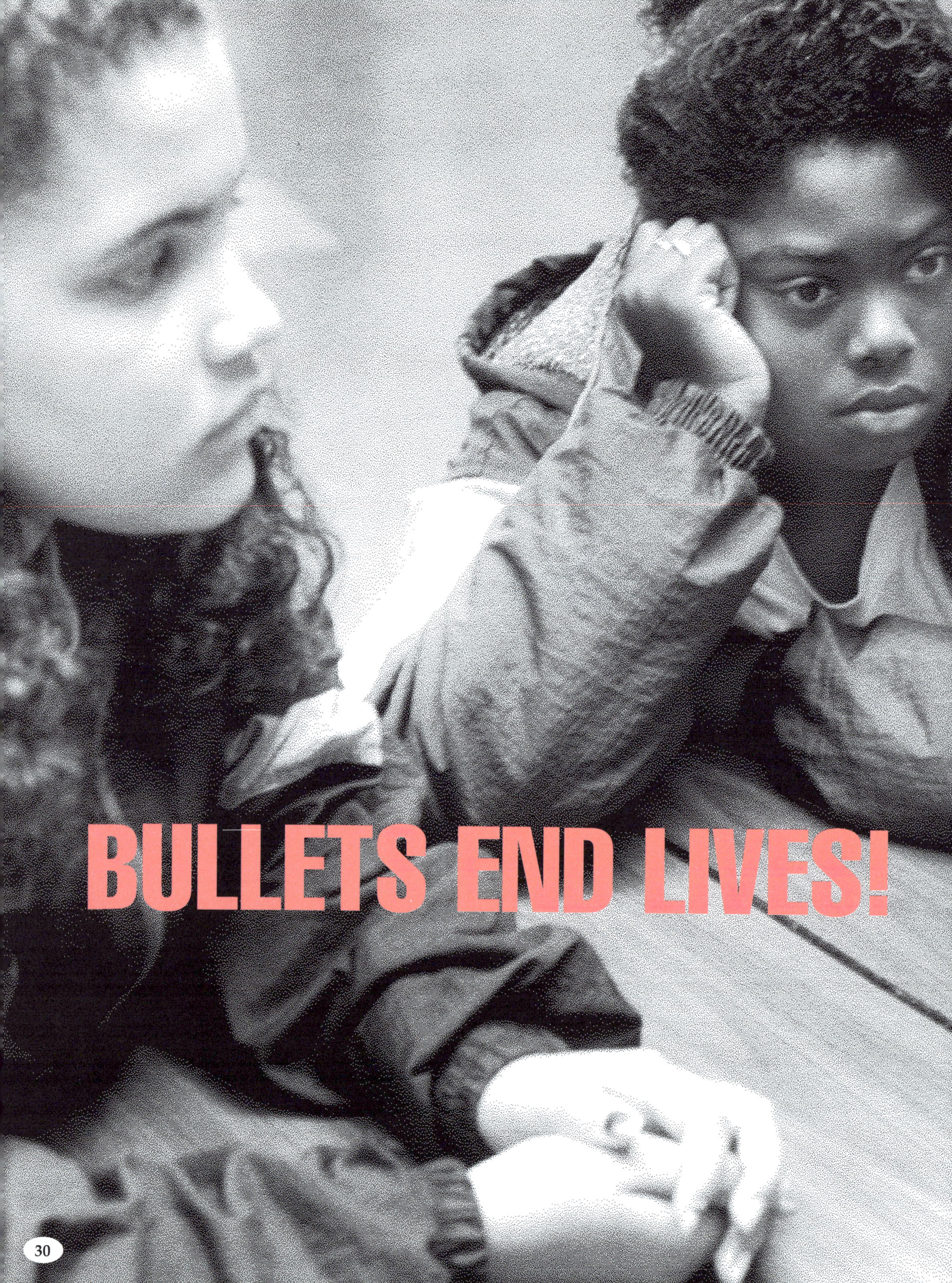

BULLETS END LIVES!

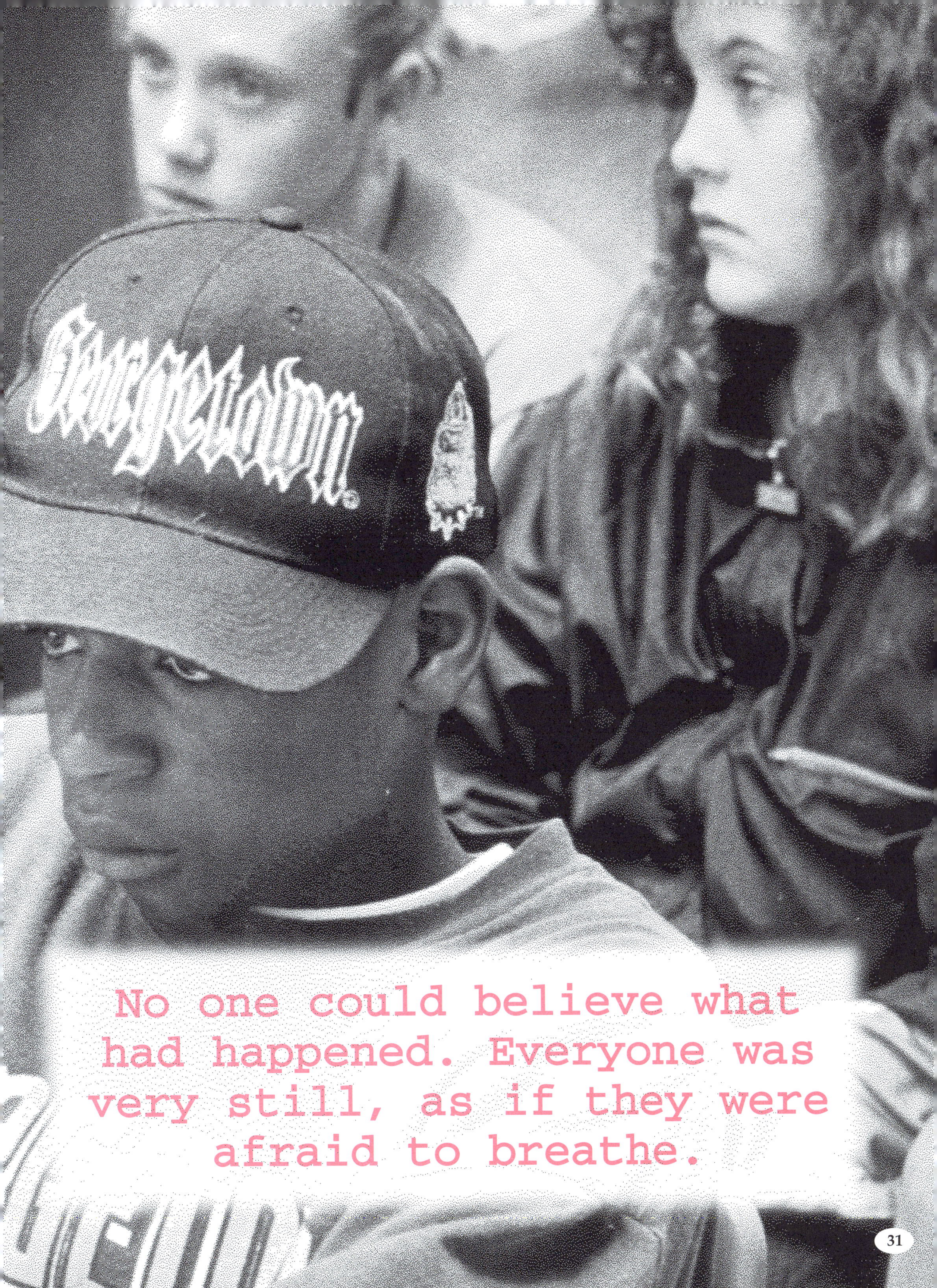

No one could believe what had happened. Everyone was very still, as if they were afraid to breathe.

Shot! With a gun!

Sophie imagined Florida's face as she tried to understand. "How could this happen to Florida?" she cried out. "Florida is just a little girl. We all love her!"

This is not TV, this is not a video game, this is not a movie. This is not a song. This is life.

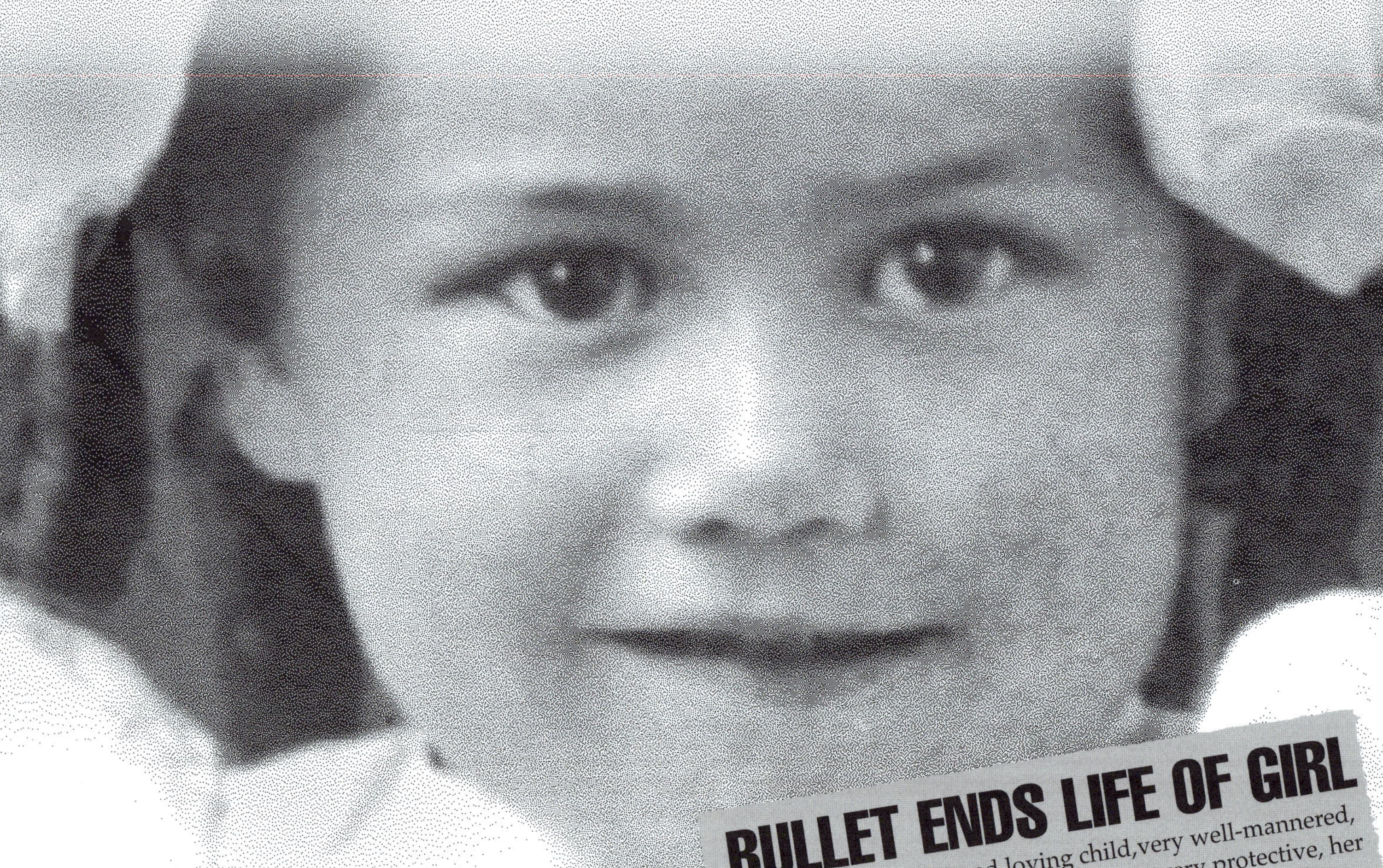

BULLET ENDS LIFE OF GIRL

"Florida was a sweet and loving child,very well-mannered, so pretty and so smart. Her mother was very protective, her father was too. Now she's gone," said a neighbor.

"It isn't fair! Please say it didn't happen to our friend!" Sophie wanted to scream.

"How could this happen to Tony?" Ricky cried out. "Tony is just a boy. We all love him. Where is Tony? I want to see him. He can't be dead. What does dead mean? Please, let me see him!" Ricky was almost hysterical.

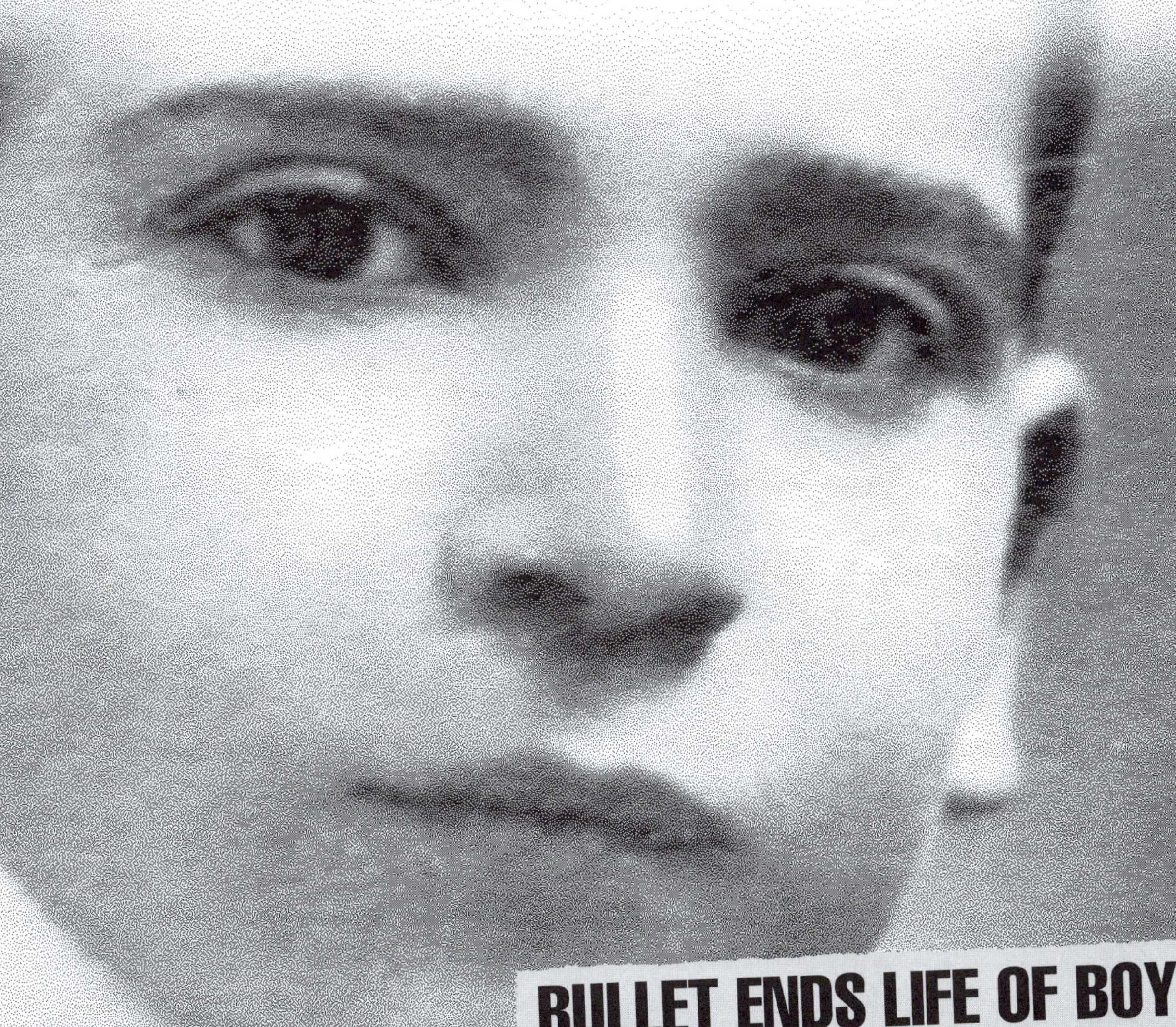

Photograph from private collection.

BULLET ENDS LIFE OF BOY

"Tony was so kind," said the boy's father. "He would often give his allowance to people who live on the streets. He wanted them to know someone cared about them. How could this happen to my son? I can't believe this. This is a parent's worst nightmare. My wife and I will never recover."

IN LOVING MEMORY

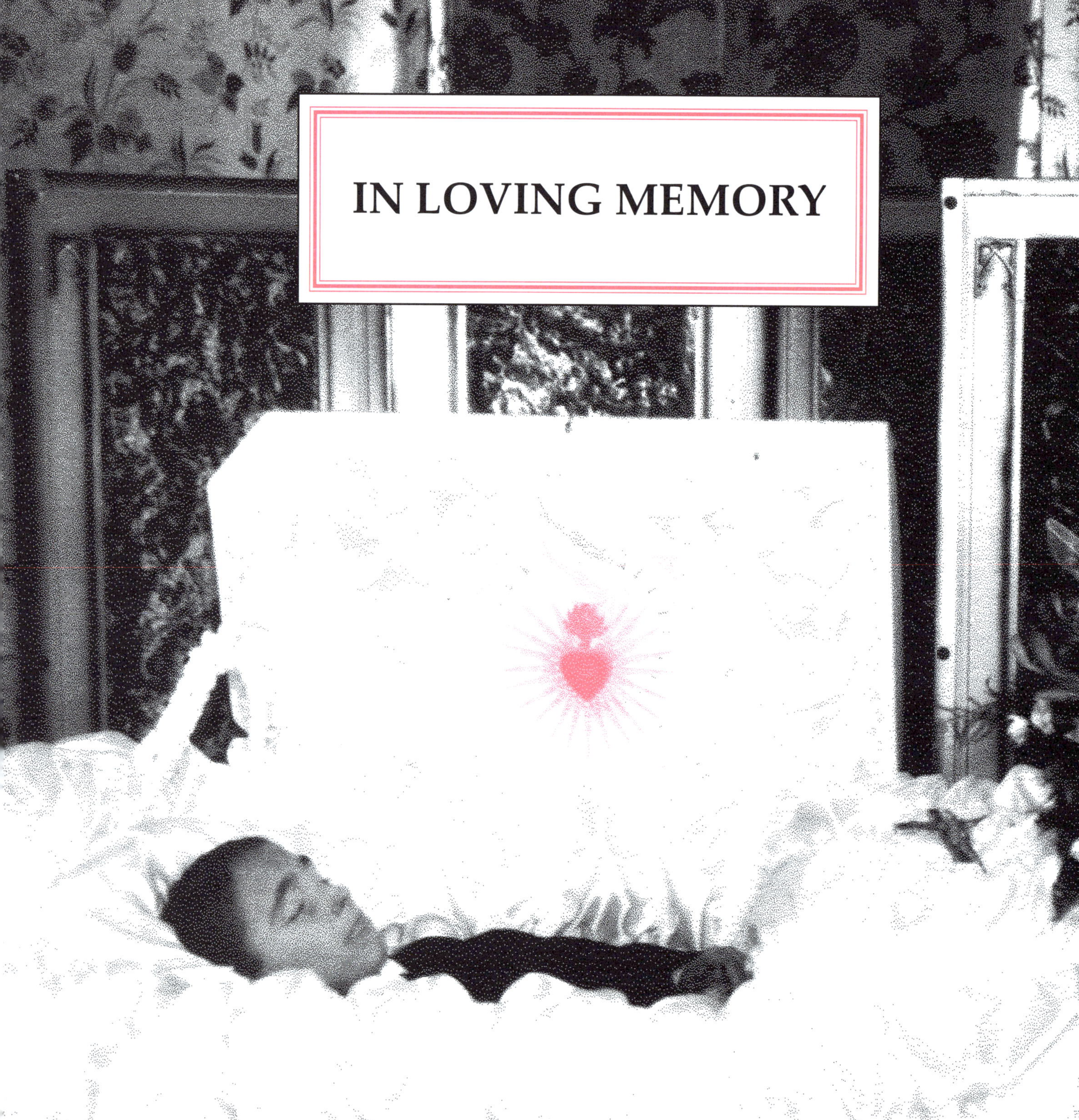

At the memorial service the clear, sweet voices of children sang Florida and Tony's favorite songs. Each child brought a flower and placed it carefully in a basket near photos of the slain children. It was hard to look at the pictures and realize that the children were now dead.

Photograph courtesy Carpenter Center for the Visual Arts, Harvard University

Ricky waited until after the service and then he went to see Tony. He wanted to talk to him. Ricky was confused as he looked at Tony. He could not *really* understand. How could his friend be dead? He must be asleep! "Make him wake up, please," Ricky cried. "Make Tony wake up!" Then he remembered hearing the gun and his ears were filled with the sounds of gunshots and sirens. Everything seemed dark. Ricky began to scream.

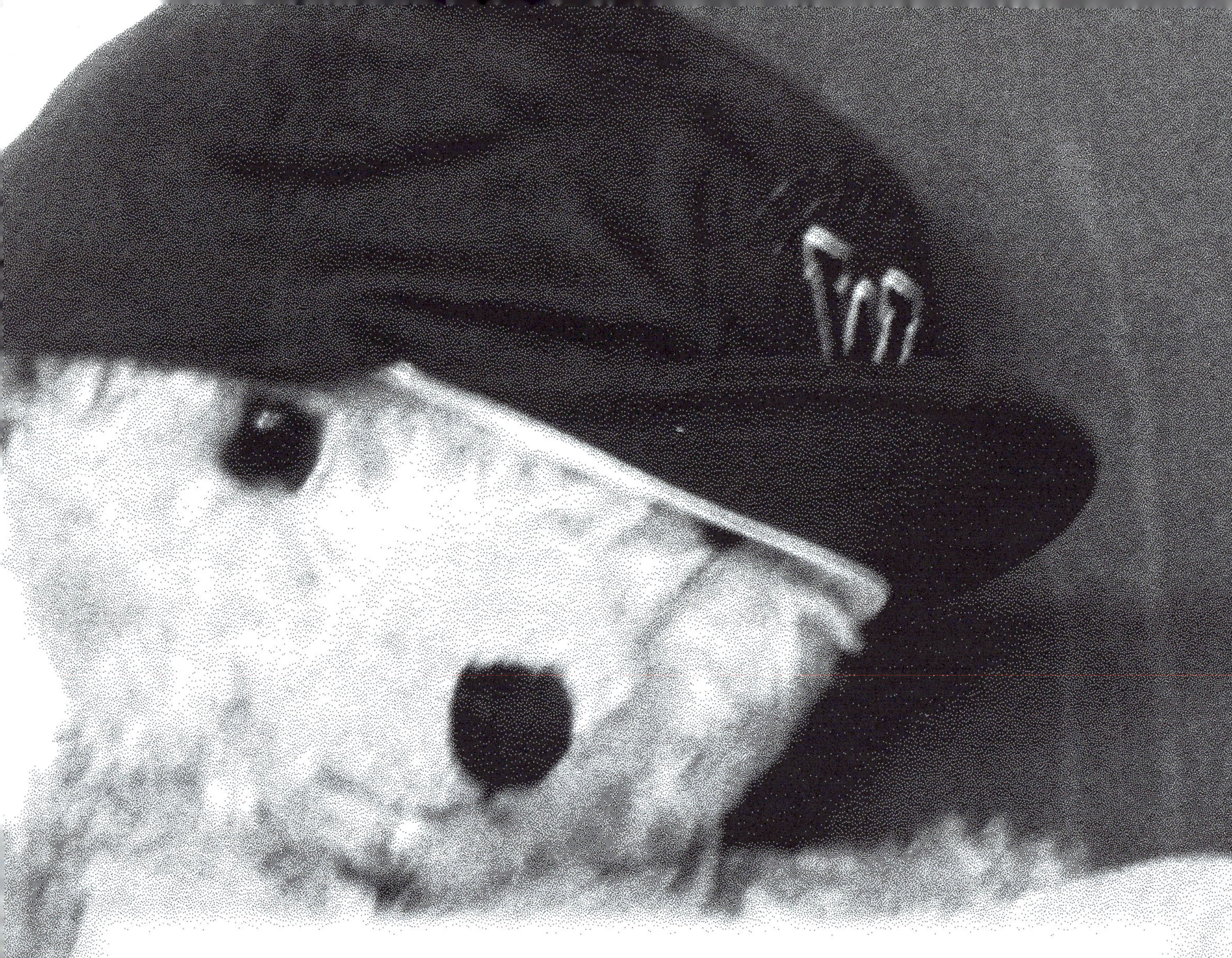

As Ricky screamed, Sophie joined in. They wanted all of America to hear them. These are the words that could be heard all over the neighborhood.

"Won't somebody stop this? GUNS KILL! Kids don't understand what death is. Why doesn't someone stop this? Please! Is there a gun nearby? Don't let it happen again. A gun could go off – please, don't let it happen."

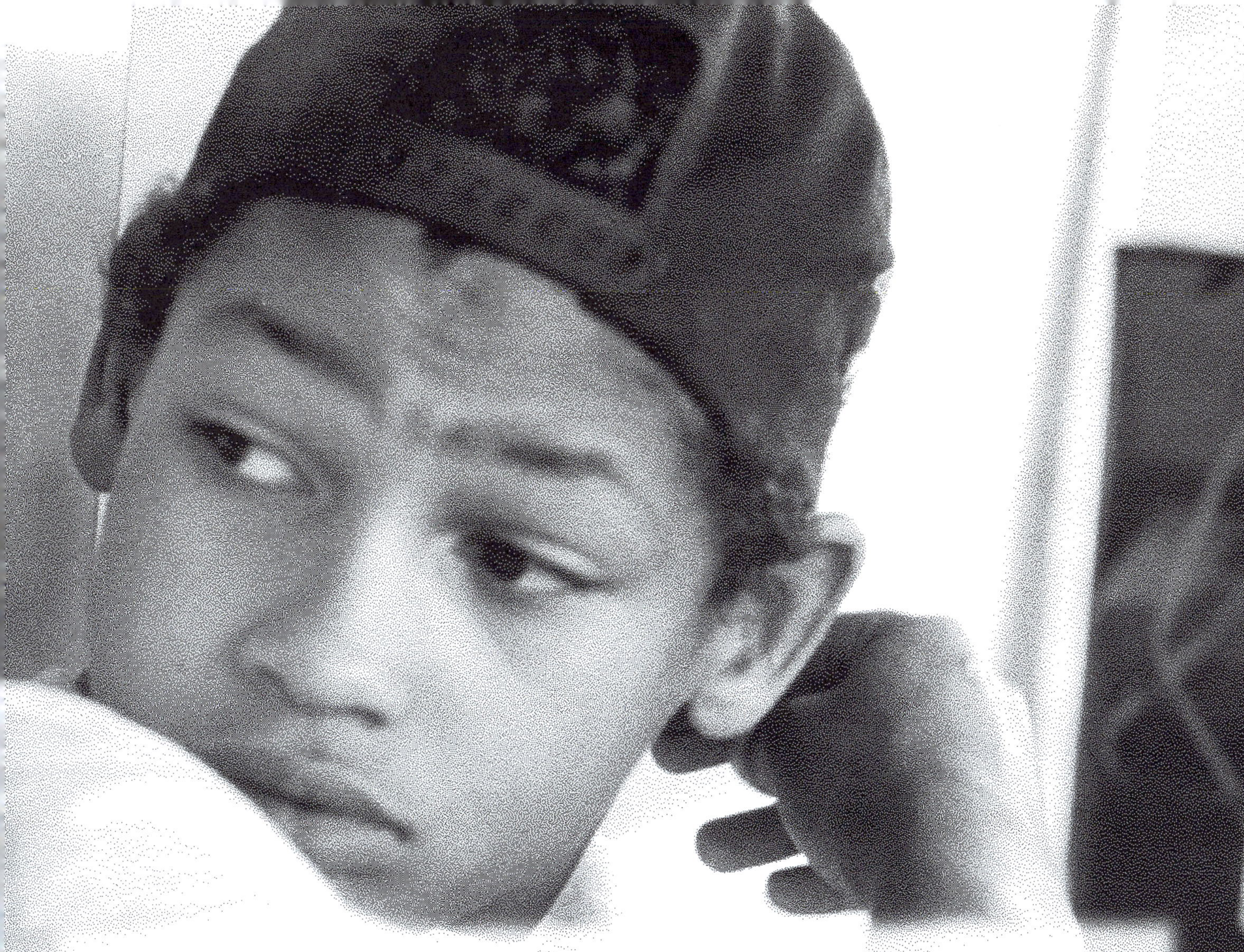

One of the big boys tried to explain how he felt. “So many people — often kids — die in shootings. Now. Everywhere, every day. Sometimes it seems we'll never live to be grown-ups.”

“Stop, don’t say that!” Ricky and Sophie cried. “It can’t be that way.”

“We have to do something,” Ricky said to Sophie. “But what? Where do we begin?”

There were so many questions to be answered. Who did this? How did it happen? Everyone wanted to know.

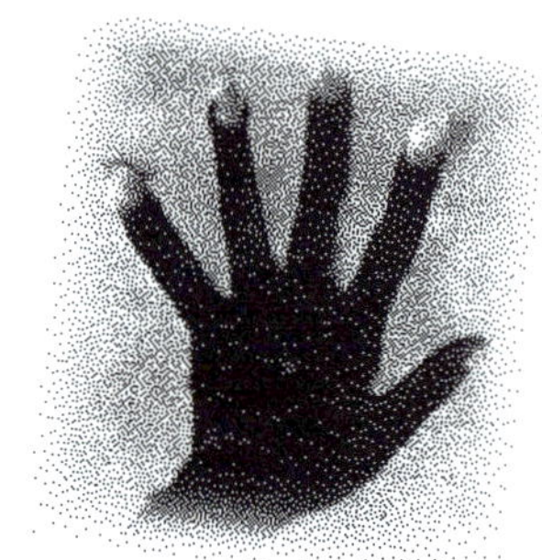

"Ask at Juvenile Hall."

"Why?"

"They'll know."

"A kid did this."

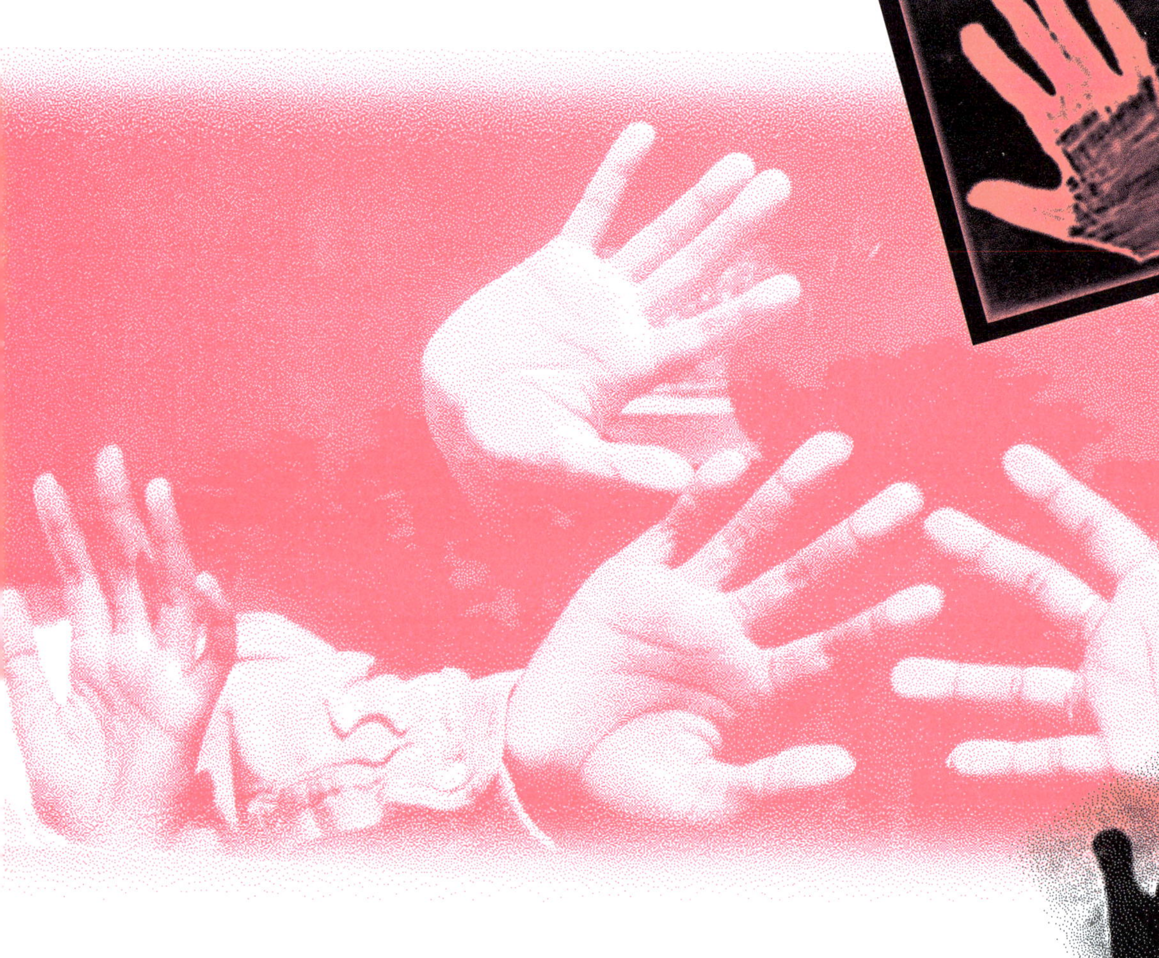

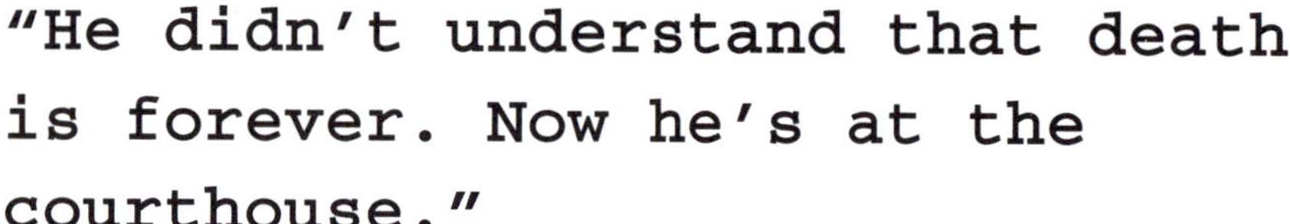

"He didn't understand that death is forever. Now he's at the courthouse."

"Why?"

"Go see for yourself."

"Go ask for the answer."

"Your Honor, how could this happen?" the boy asked.

"Easy – there was a gun," answered the judge.

"How did the kid get it?" asked Ricky.

"Easy," said the judge again.

"We don't understand – isn't there a law?" asked the boy.

The judge smiled. "What does a gun know about the law?"

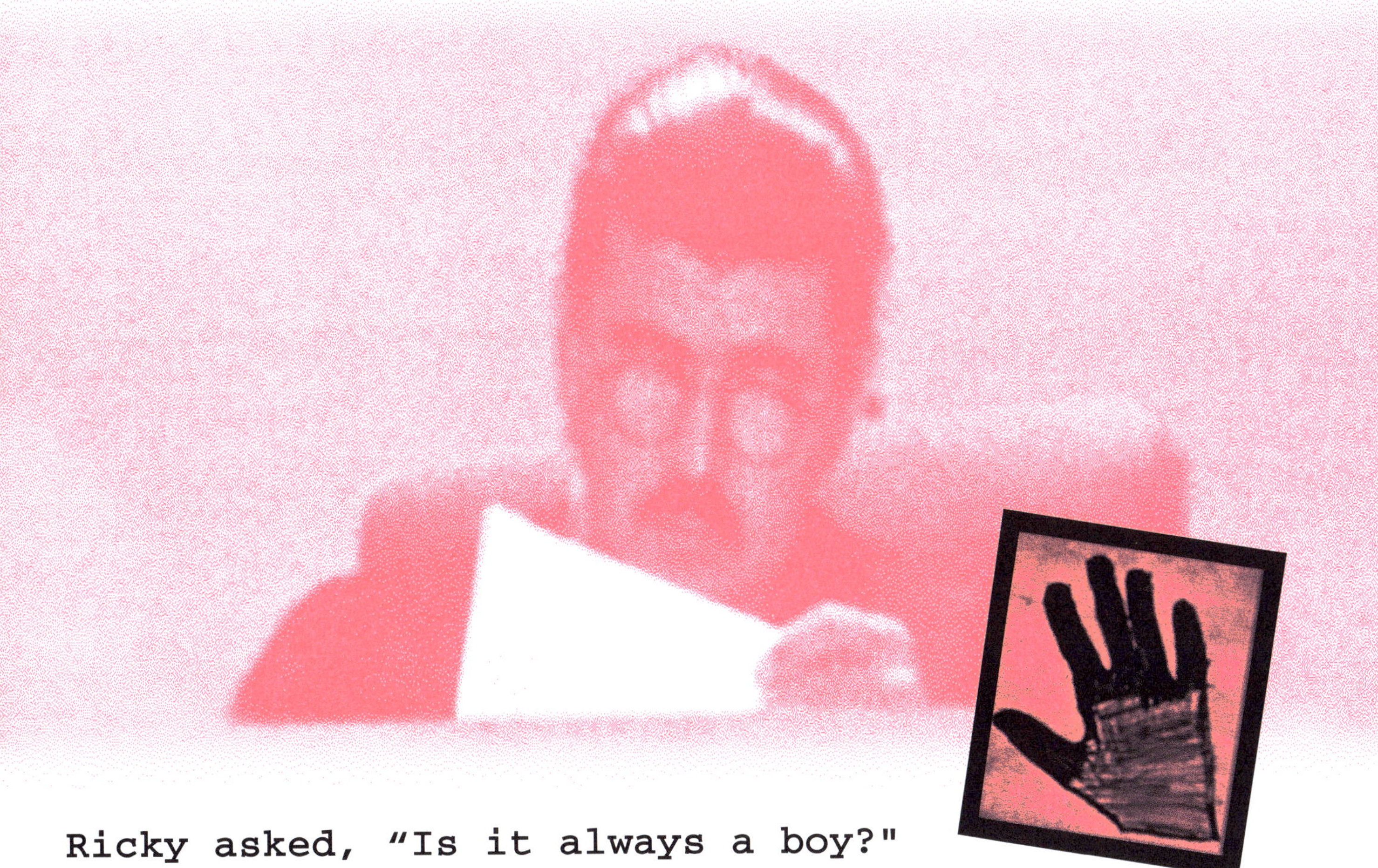

Ricky asked, "Is it always a boy?"

"No," said the judge. "Sometimes it's a girl, sometimes a teenager, sometimes an adult. Sometimes it's an accident, but guns kill!"

The victims' family sat silently.

The defendant's family expressed their sorrow for the victims' family. They wished they could change what had happened, but no one could.

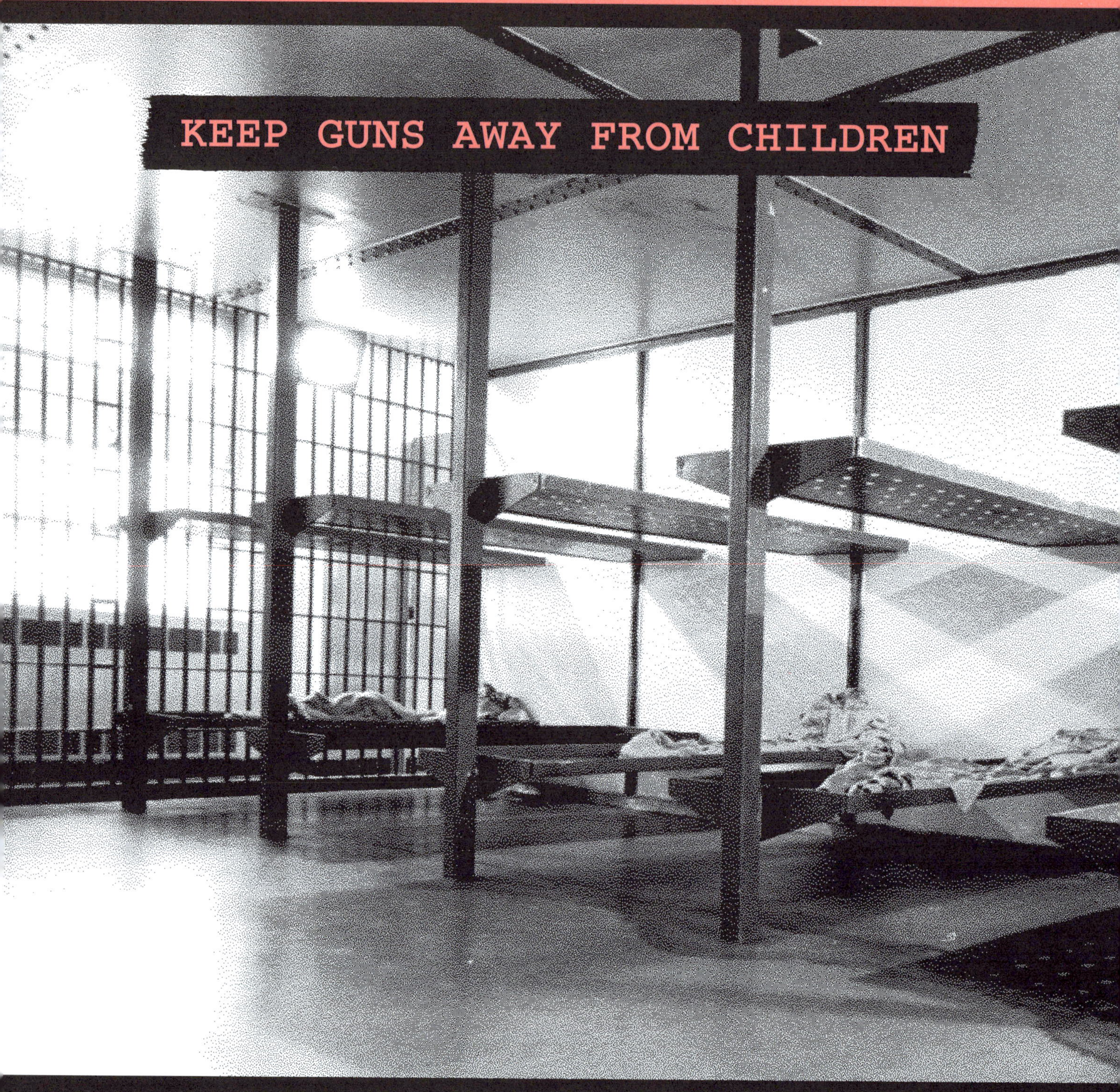

The judge let the kids and the bears visit the jail. They had to talk to the kid who had the gun. They had to ask him why he did it. They couldn't understand why someone would play with a gun.

Families shattered by violence

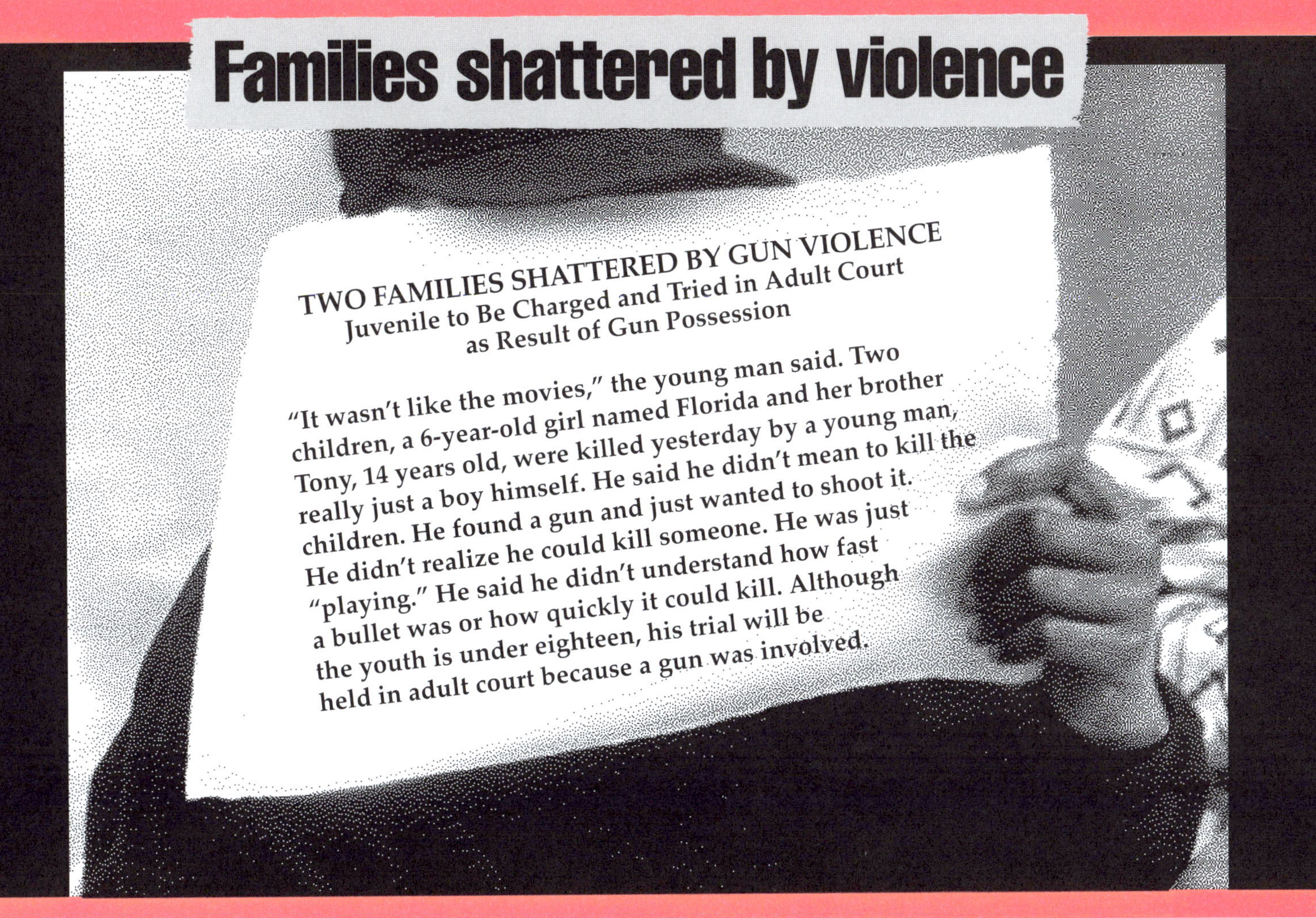

TWO FAMILIES SHATTERED BY GUN VIOLENCE
Juvenile to Be Charged and Tried in Adult Court
as Result of Gun Possession

"It wasn't like the movies," the young man said. Two children, a 6-year-old girl named Florida and her brother Tony, 14 years old, were killed yesterday by a young man, really just a boy himself. He said he didn't mean to kill the children. He found a gun and just wanted to shoot it. He didn't realize he could kill someone. He was just "playing." He said he didn't understand how fast a bullet was or how quickly it could kill. Although the youth is under eighteen, his trial will be held in adult court because a gun was involved.

"Why did you do it? What were you thinking?" asked one of Florida and Tony's friends. "You're just a kid yourself."

The young man in jail cried, "I'm sorry. I didn't know what death was. I didn't realize that the gun would destroy two people – that their family will never be the same and neither will mine. Forgive me! I'm only a kid. Please, how can I undo what I did? I didn't mean to. I'm so sorry! Please, please help me. Forgive me."

The boy and the young man cried. They cried for Florida and Tony. They cried for all the mothers and fathers. They cried for all the families and friends. They cried for themselves. But all their crying will never change what happened.

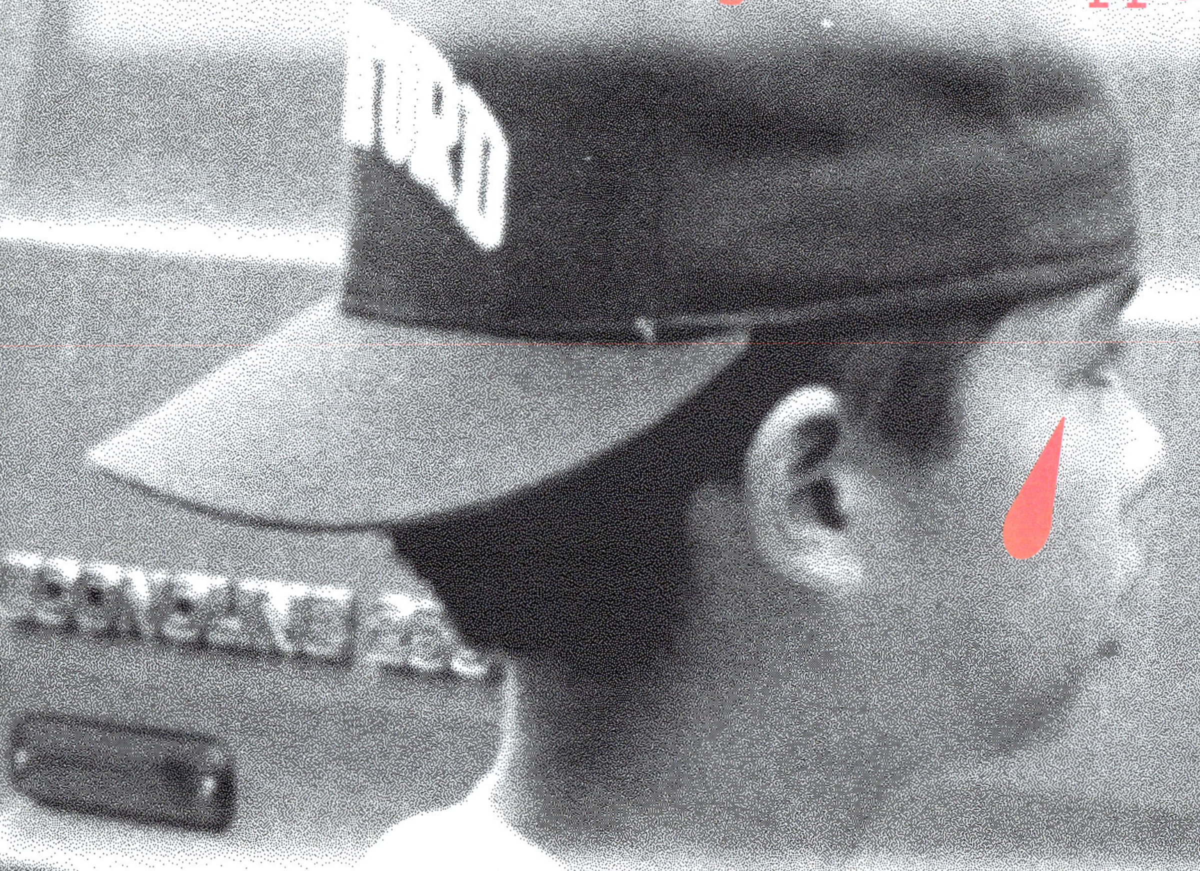

The boy said good-bye to the young man. The young man carefully picked up Ricky and Sophie and they said good-bye to him. Before he handed Ricky back to the boy, the young man buried his face in the teddy bear's fur. No one knew what to say or do. The children and the bears silently left the jail.

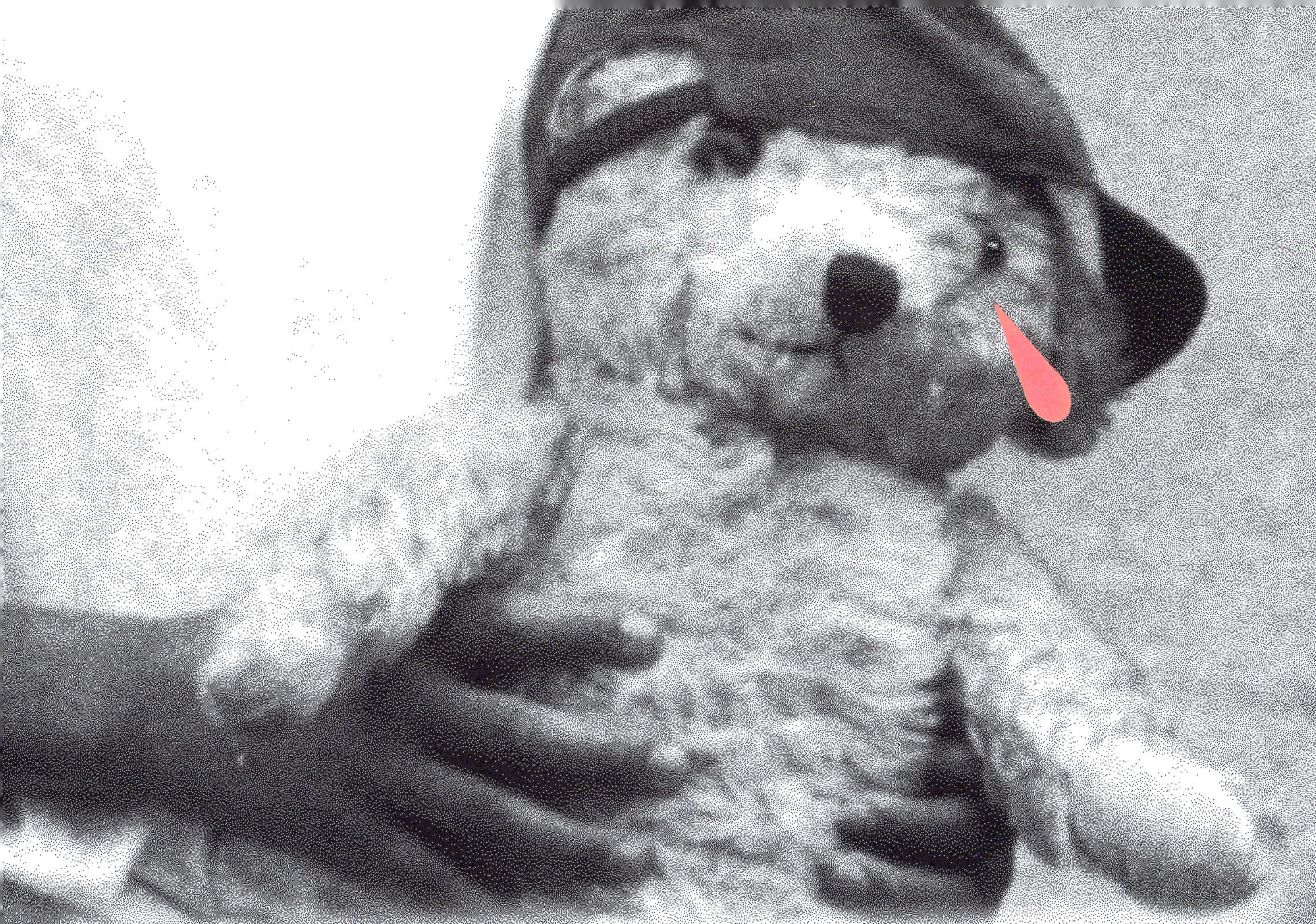

Ricky was very angry. He could hardly breathe. He tried to explain how he felt. "It's not fair. Kids make mistakes. Kids are just kids. Now Florida and Tony are dead." He began to cry.

How could people let this happen? How could they let kids have guns? Bears, real bears, protect their cubs. Teddy bears always love and comfort children. Why don't people think of children, all the children? Don't they care?

Ricky and Sophie felt sad without the love and life of the children. They were angry at the loss of Florida and Tony. They were angry because their friends were filled with grief, and the sorrow seemed never ending.

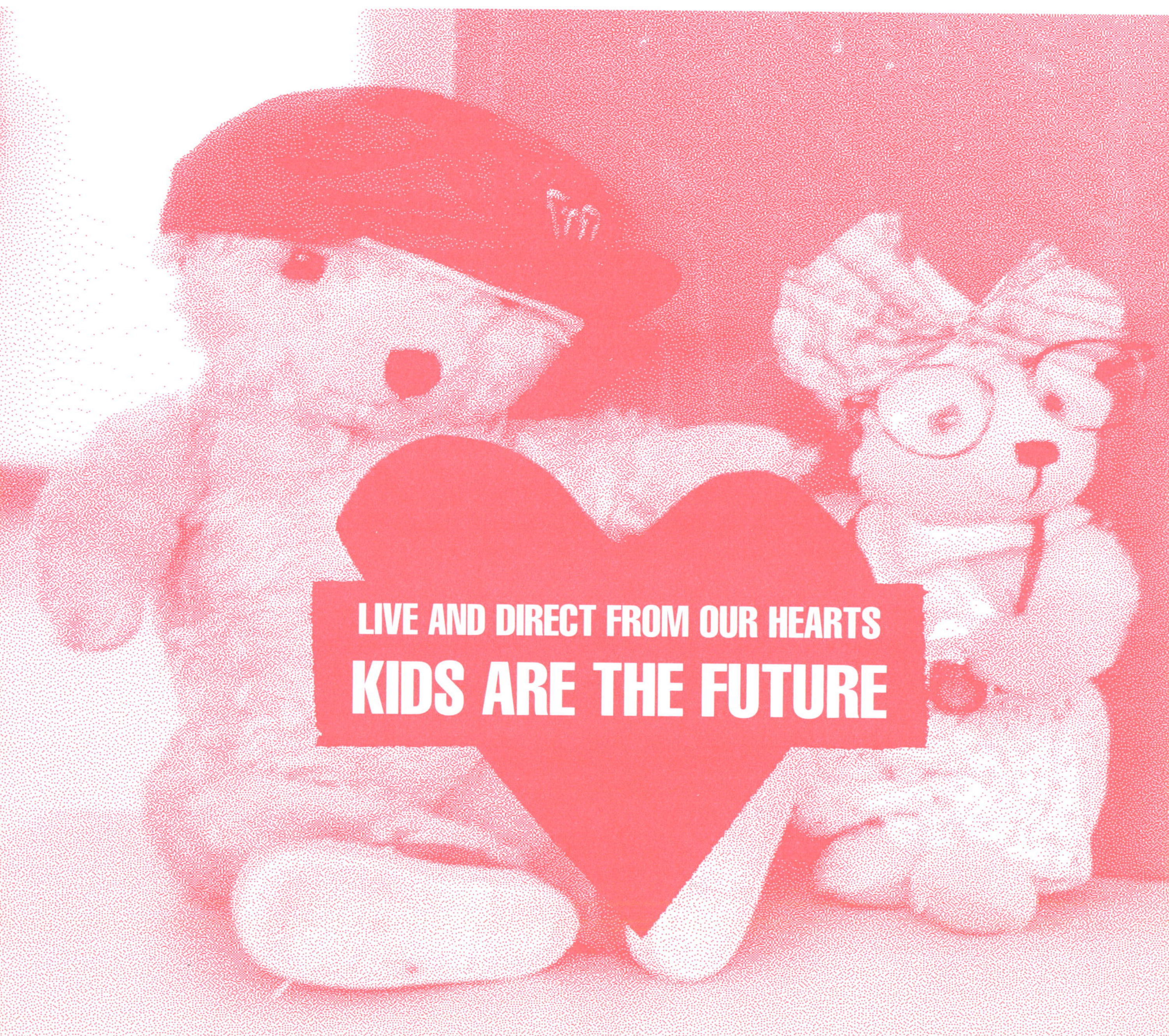

"We have to do something," Sophie said. "Listen up — we have to do something to help the children. Let's make a brighter world for all of the children."

STOP THE VIOLENCE *PLEASE*

"We'll all do something!" the boy said. "We'll make posters and postcards to tell everyone to stop the violence. We want everyone to live."

All the kids joined together with Ricky and Sophie. They used colored chalk to outline and color drawings of their hands and paws. Hand in hand, they asked others to unite with them in trying to stop the violence.

Everyone they asked to help said yes. Everyone wanted to stop the violence, to protect the children and protect the future.

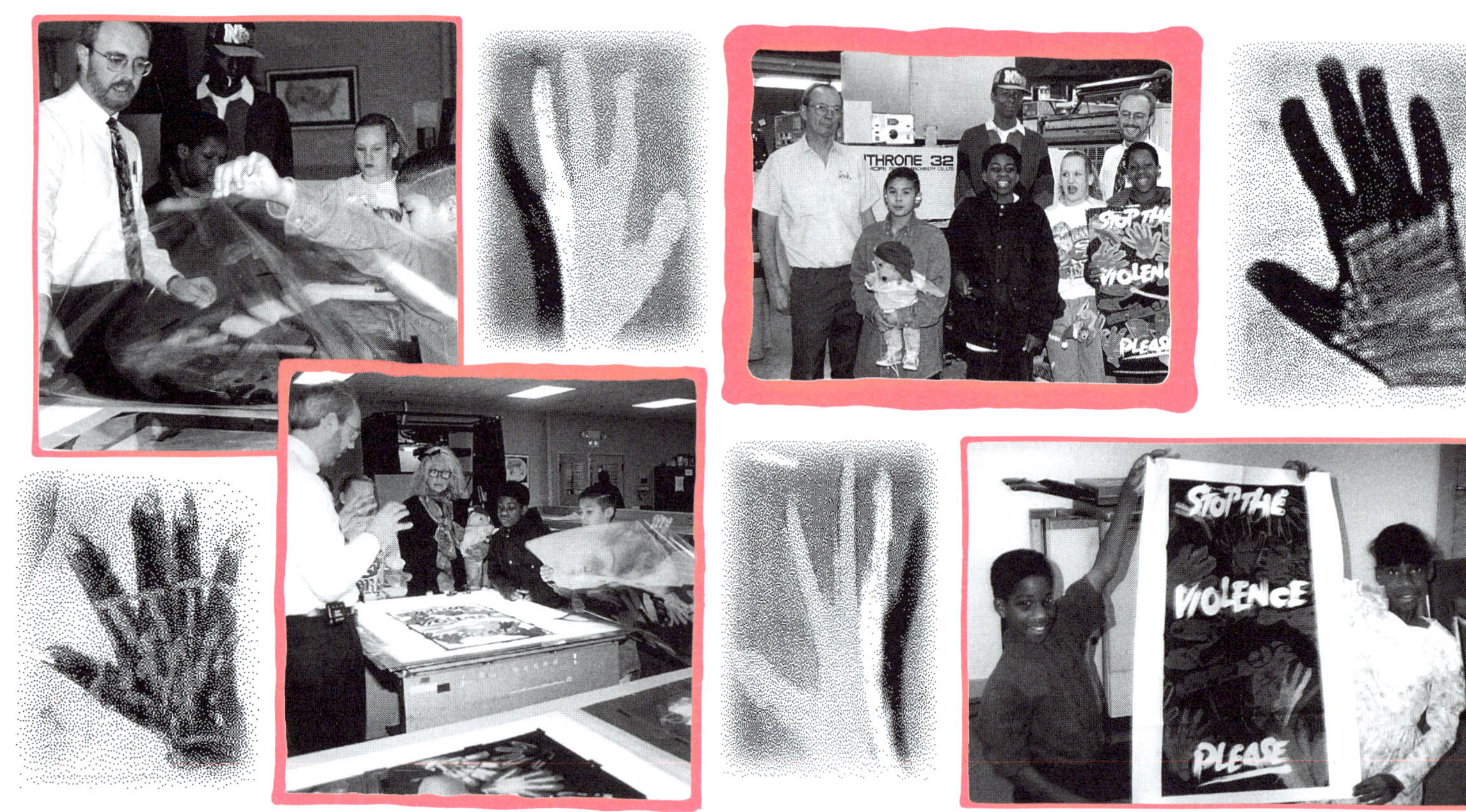

Their poster design included the image of a gun. Some adults worried that it might terrify children or, even worse, make the gun seem cool. They suggested removing the gun. After Florida and Tony's friends discussed the poster with various groups and ages of kids — from second graders to a council made up of young gang members — everyone knew the gun had to stay.

The gang members suggested putting a brush stroke through the gun. They said that everyone would know what that meant, even if they could not read English.

Kids who saw the poster said, "Kids are smart enough to know that this poster doesn't glamorize the gun, and the image doesn't scare us. We can figure it out. We're confronted with this every day. Adults keep talking about it. They talk *at* us, but they can't seem to talk *with* us. Maybe this poster will help adults to think more about what violence does to children."

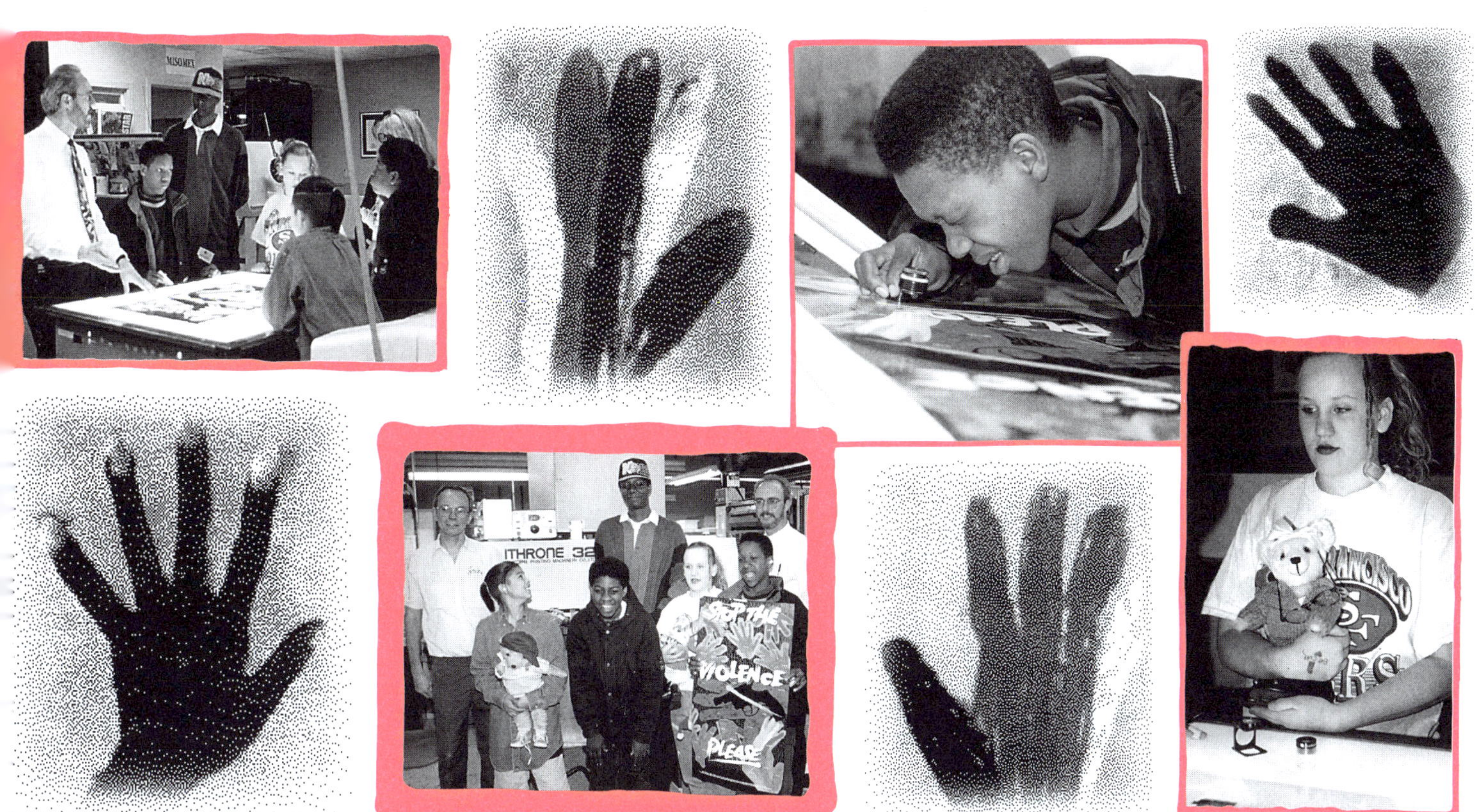

NOW IS THE TIME—INCREASE THE PEACE

LIVE AND DIRECT

TEAMWORK WILL MAKE THE DREAM WORK

They had copies of the poster printed. Ricky took one to City Hall and Sophie took some to the libraries. The kids took posters to their schools. The poster began to have a life of its own. It inspired others to create "Increase the Peace" banners which were hung in schools.

The tall boy talked on the radio about stopping the violence and the big boy told his story in rap.

Another boy and his father wrote a song. Maybe someday you'll hear it on your radio.

Until then, Peace, from Ricky, Sophie, and the "Live and Direct Kids." Please join them to help stop the violence and increase the peace.

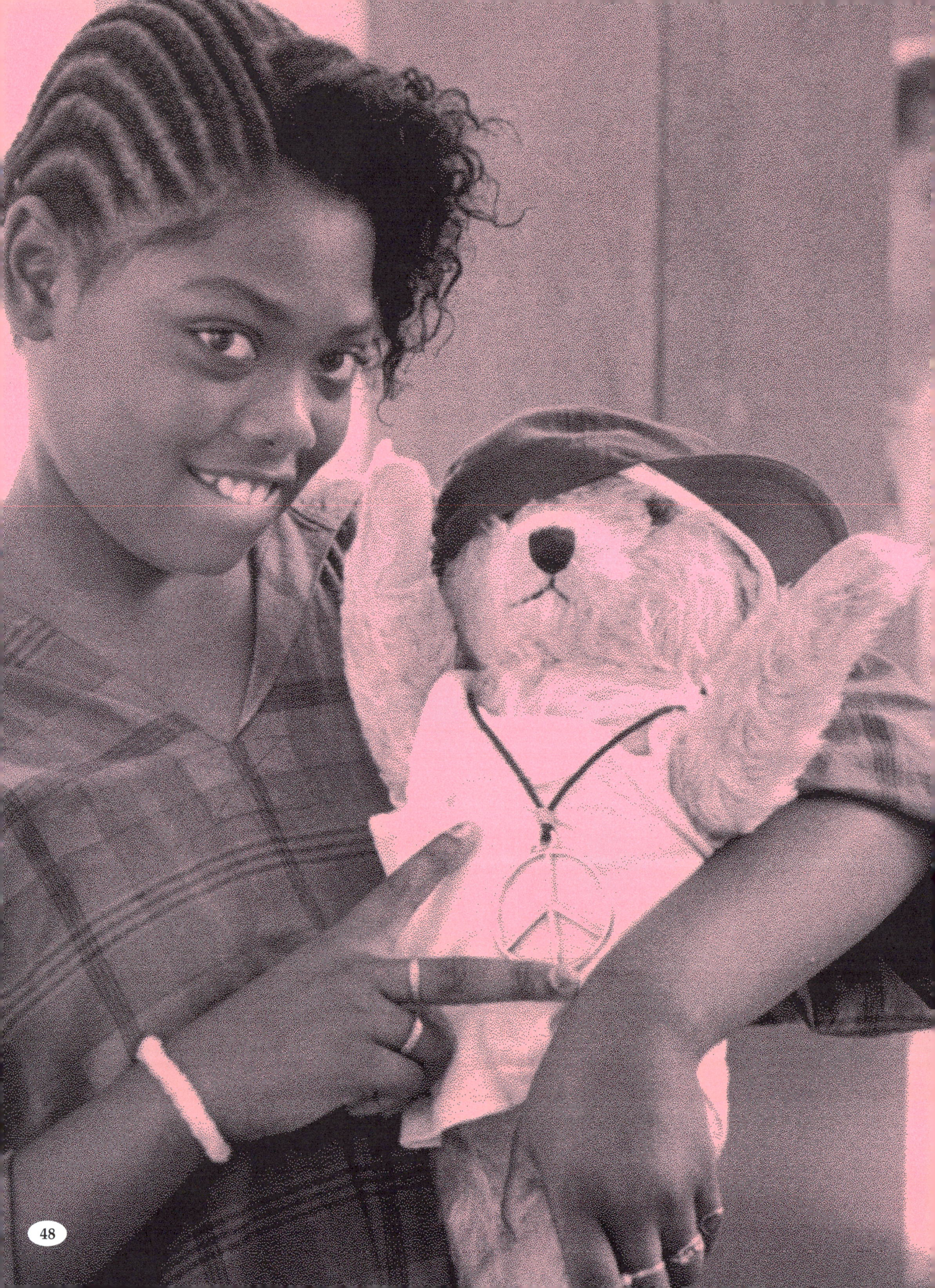

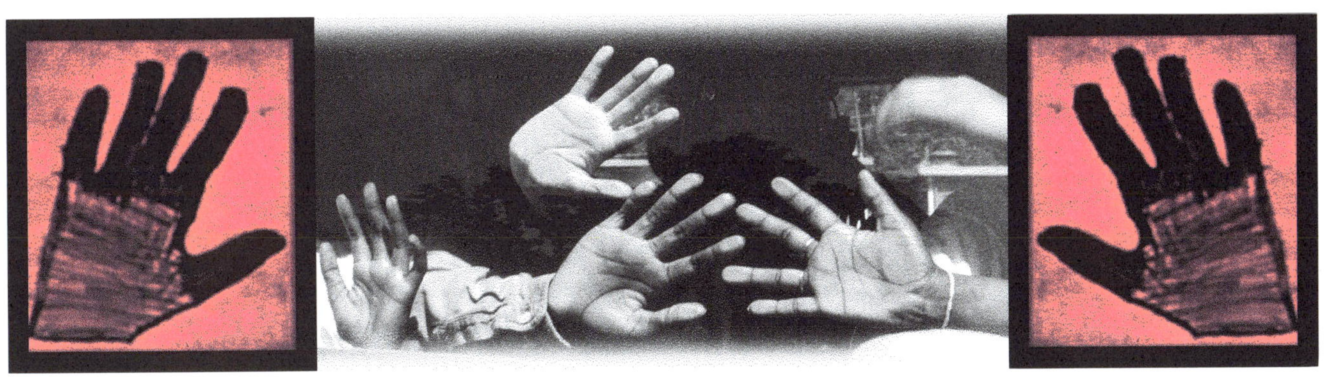

Taking Action

Resources for Parents and Kids

Get Involved & Involve the Kids

Call the mayor, call the governor, call the president, call your council person, call the TV stations, call the radio stations, call the newspapers, call the National Rifle Association, call the gun manufacturers, call the gun clubs, involve the libraries. Talk the talk *and* walk the walk. If not now, when? Vote (register if you haven't already) for school bonds and levies. Write letters. Go to city hall. Work on legislation. Call a meeting. Plan a demonstration. Shout! March! Think of what's happening today. What will it be like in five years? Ten years?

Look in the mirror. Look in your house. Open your eyes. Hold out your hand. The future is now.

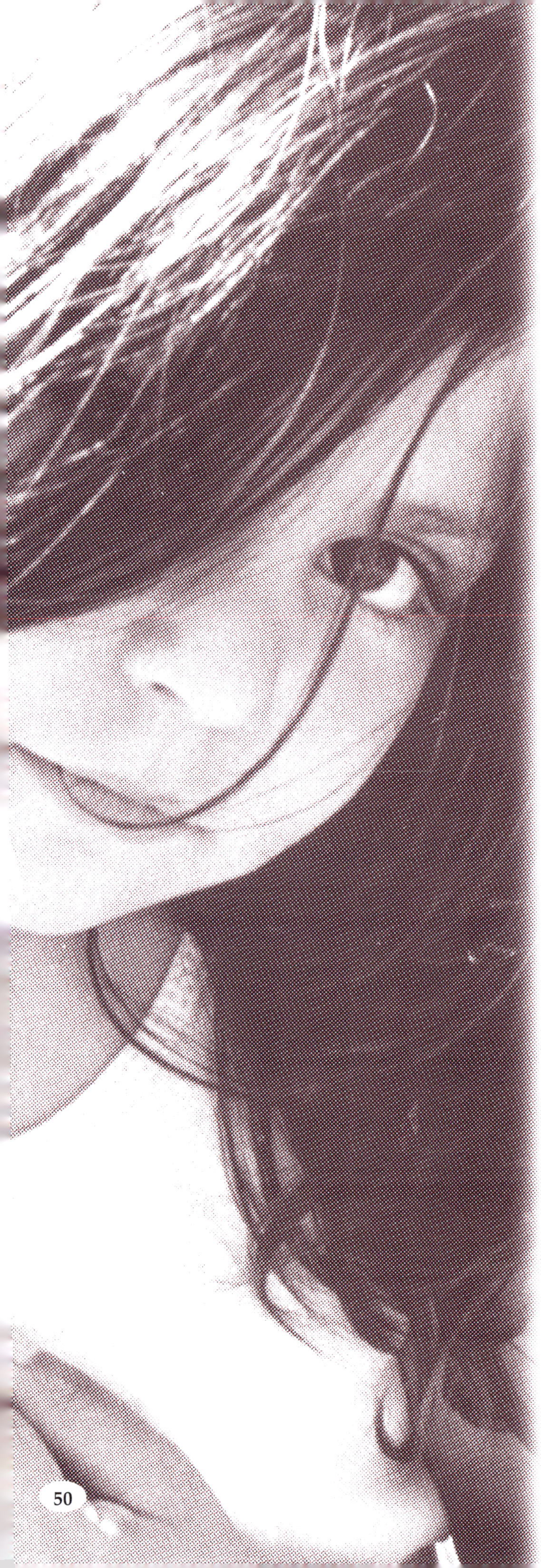

Facts and Actions

Gunshot Wounds

Deadly Equations:

1. energy, mass, velocity

$$E = \frac{mv^2}{2}$$

2. violence, guns, death

$$\frac{V + G + D}{\text{FOREVER}}$$

When a bullet smashes into the body, it brings *hundreds, sometimes thousands* of foot-pounds of energy with it. This causes the bullet to crush the flesh and bone as it passes through the body.

A bullet from an assault rifle tears through the tissue, snagging everything in its wake, and exits through a gaping hole. Assault weapons were made for war—to maim and kill humans. Treatment of the wounds they produce requires the services of a level one trauma center. These guns are now on the streets of America, often in the hands of children.

Assault weapons produce wounds of unbelievable destruction that require extensive surgical repair. If a person has been shot in the arm or leg with a high-velocity gun, the injury may be severe enough to require amputation. Most gunshot wounds are due to handguns, which are lower velocity but can cause deadly wounds, especially at close range.

Sometimes children are caught in crossfire. Terrified and screaming, they are brought to emergency rooms for life-saving care and treatment. Children are *not small adults*—by the time they look physically bad—

pale, quiet, or gray from blood loss, they are in a *lot of trouble* and need immediate surgery and / or blood replacement. Life-saving intervention often overwhelms a child or teenager in the critical "golden hour"—the first hour of medical care after trauma.

Many gunshot wounds cause serious blood loss. This can be due to laceration of organs such as the liver, spleen, kidneys, or stomach. When a bullet perforates an intestine, the contents of the bowel spills into the abdominal cavity, usually causing severe infection. A bullet injury to the brain may make the patient paralyzed or comatose. Gunshot wounds to the back may hit the spine, causing instant and often permanent paralysis.

These are the real consequences of gunshots! It is not like the movies or TV.

Help Save a Life

Become a volunteer blood donor. One donation can help three different patients. Anyone who is in good health, is at least 18 years old (persons 16 or 17 years old may donate with written consent of their legal guardian) and weighs at least 110 pounds may donate blood every 56 days.

Potential donors complete a thorough health-screening evaluation to determine eligibility. The evaluation includes a medical history assessment and a brief physical examination of blood pressure, pulse, and temperature, and a test for anemia. Donors are asked several questions concerning HIV risk.

Inquire at your local blood bank about organizing a school or workplace blood campaign. Teenagers as well as adults can participate in this community gift-giving.

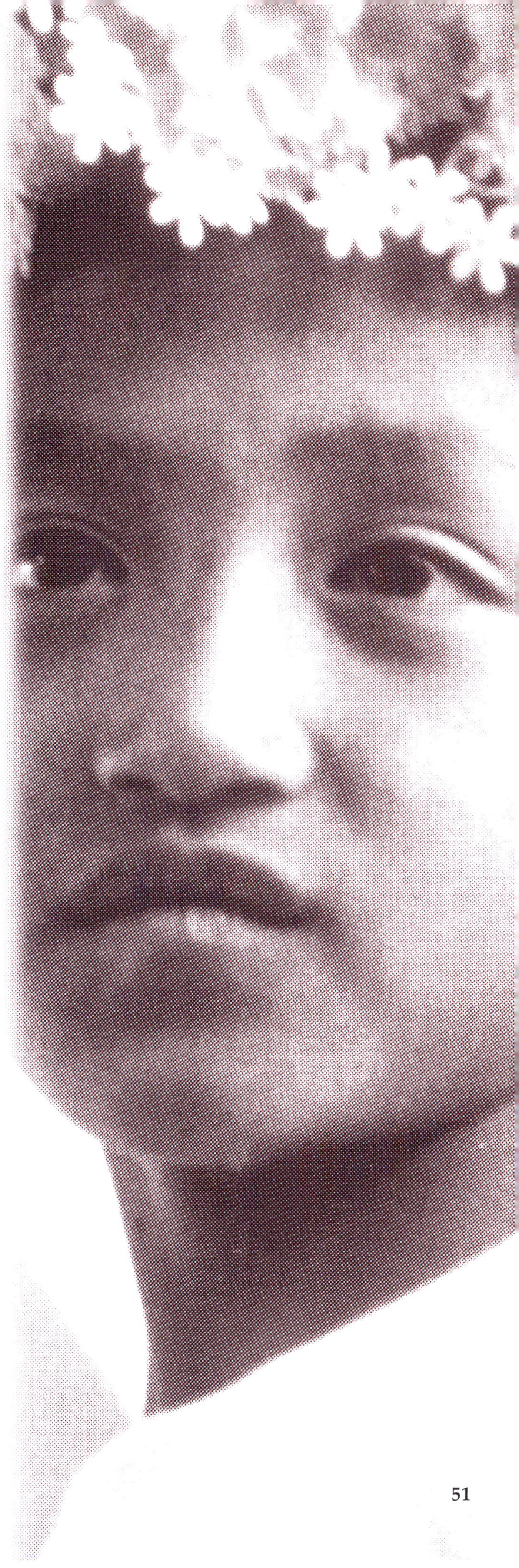

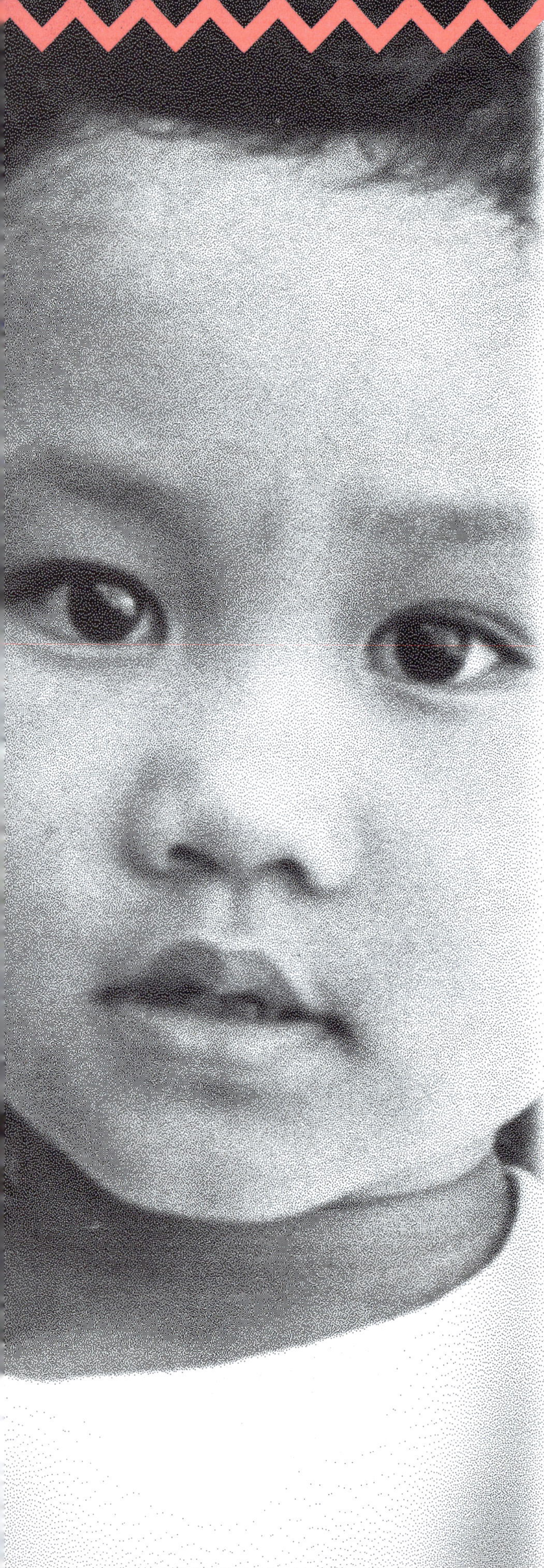

Facts Entered in the U.S. Senate

According to the Centers for Disease Control, an estimated 34,000 Americans die from firearm injuries each year, including 25,000 from handgun violence.

Firearms rank as the eighth leading cause of death in the United States, and less than 5 percent of fatal shootings are unintentional.

The National Center for Health Statistics reported in March 1993 that, among Americans age 15 through 24, firearms are the cause of more deaths than all natural causes combined.

From 1979 to 1989, the firearm homicide rate among children age 15 through 19 increased 61 percent, while the nonfirearm homicide rate fell 29 percent.

More than 135,000 students carry handguns to school every day. An additional 270,000 students have carried a gun to school at least once.

The United States leads industrialized nations in the percentage of households with firearms and the number of homicides with guns. . . .

According to the 1991 Advisory Council on Social Security, the overall annual cost of firearms injury to the health care system in the United States is more than $4 billion.

Public funds pay for an estimated 85 percent of the cost of hospitalization for firearm injuries, excluding professional fees and the cost of ambulance, physical therapy, and other rehabilitative services.

The indirect costs of gun-related injuries, such as disability payments, legal fees, and lost work time, are estimated to be two times the estimated annual direct cost of firearm injury.

U.S. Senate Bill 868, May 4, 1993

Children and Guns

Young people between the ages of 15 and 24 are at highest risk of committing and experiencing violence. Youth violence is increasing at an alarming rate.

"A Preliminary Assessment of Violence in Washington State," Washington State Department of Health, Injury Prevention Program, November 1993

In 1991, gun accidents were the fifth leading cause of accidental death for children ages 14 and under.

"Accident Facts," National Safety Council, 1992

Every day in America, 14 children ages 19 and under are killed in gun accidents, suicides, and homicides. Many more are wounded.

In 1990, 2,874 children and teenagers were murdered with guns, 1,476 committed suicide with guns, and 541 died in unintentional shootings.

Firearm homicide is the leading cause of death for black men aged 15–34.

In 1990, 1,416 people were accidentally killed with firearms.

Firearms kill more people between the ages of 15 and 24 than all natural causes combined. Firearms are the number two killer of men and women 10–34 years of age—second only to motor vehicle crashes.

Firearm injuries, fatal and nonfatal combined, are the third most costly type of injury overall. Data from 1985 suggest a total national cost of $14.4 billion in lifetime costs, which increased to at least $16.2 billion by 1988.

The average per-person cost of firearm fatalities is the highest of any injury-related death, at $373,000 per death.

Lois A. Fingerhut, "Firearm Mortality among Children, Youth, and Young Adults 1–34 Years of Age, Trends and Current Status: United States, 1985–90," Advance Data no. 231 (Hyattsville, Md.: National Center for Health Statistics, 1993)

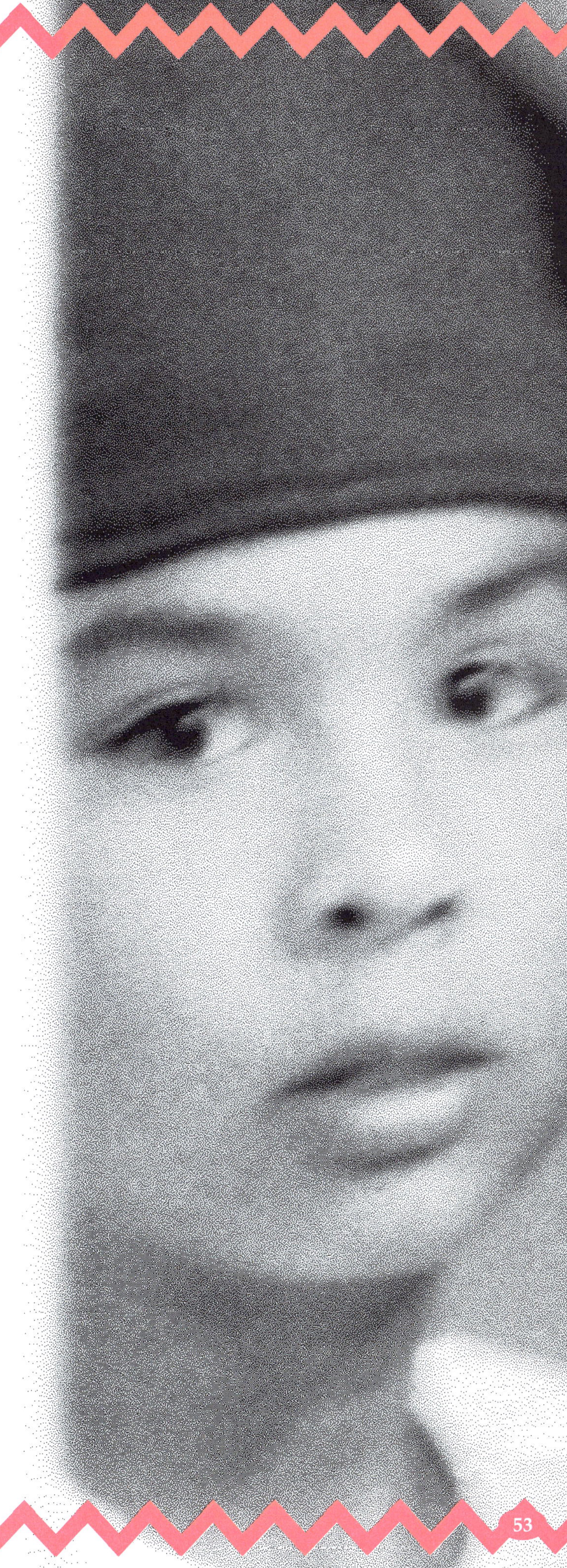

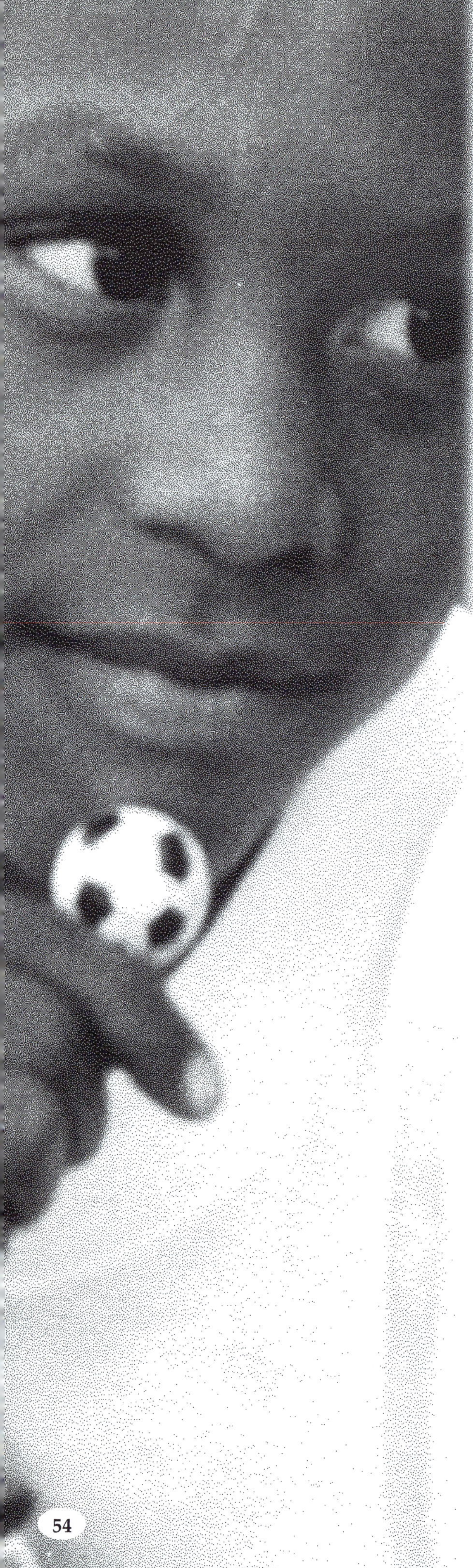

Wave of the Future

Guns Will Eclipse Cars as Leading Cause of Death Unless We Stop the Violence

If current trends continue, gunshot wounds will take more lives nationally than automobile accidents by 2003—a point already reached in the District of Columbia and six states, including New York, according to a report released today by the Department of Health and Human Services.

New York Times, *January 27, 1994*

In order to put firearms as a cause of death into perspective, causes of death for children, teenagers, and young adults have been reordered in an alternative ranking scheme that includes detailed causes of injury.

Based on this new ranking, firearms are the second leading cause of death (after motor vehicle injury fatalities) for children 10–14 years of age, teenagers 15–19 years of age, and young adults 20–24 years and 25–34 years of age. For persons 15–19 and 20–24 years of age, firearm homicide as an individual category of death was second only to motor vehicle deaths.

Among black males, firearm injuries were the leading cause of death among children 10–14 through adults 25–34 years of age. For children 10–14 years, firearms were responsible for 30 percent more deaths than motor vehicle injuries. For black males 15–19 through 20–24 years, firearm homicide was the single leading cause of death, with more than three times the number of motor vehicle deaths. Firearm homicide was also the leading cause of death at ages 25–34 years.

The firearm homicide rates among young persons 15–19 and 20–24 years continue to increase and the rates of increase have recently worsened for white males. For young black males 15–19 and 20–24 years of age, the average annual increases in firearm homicide of 20 percent and 15 percent, respectively, observed from 1985 to 1988 remained unchanged through 1988 to 1990. For white males 15–19 years, the firearm homicide rate increased an average of 4 percent per year from 1985 through 1988 and remained unchanged for those 20–24 years, whereas the firearm homicide rate increased at average annual rates of 24 percent and 12 percent for white males 15–19 and 20–24 years, respectively, from 1988 through 1990. Not only is progress not being made in reducing the rate of increase in firearm homicide for these young black males, but attention must also be paid to increasing firearm homicide rates among young white males.

Lois A Fingerhut, "Firearm Mortality among Children, Youth and Young Adults 1–34 Years of Age, Trends and Current Status: United States, 1985–90," Advance Data no. 231, (Hyattsville, Md.: National Center for Health Statistics, 1993)

The number of handgun-related incidents in elementary and secondary schools has increased sharply, with significant numbers of school children in rural and urban areas reporting easy access to and frequent carrying to school of handguns; and the presence of handguns in school not only provokes worry among parents and children but also causes much-needed school funds to be diverted for purchase of security equipment.

U.S. Senate Bill 892, May 4, 1993

A Harris poll of 2,508 schoolchildren, published on July 20th, suggests that guns are startlingly common in American schools. Almost a tenth of those interviewed admitted that they had shot at someone at some time in their lives, and 11 percent said that they had been shot at in the past year. Nearly 40 percent said they knew someone who had been killed or injured by a gun, and 15 percent that they had carried a gun within the past 30 days. Although some experts find these figures a trifle high (youthful bravado doubtless inflated them), everyone agrees that, when it comes to juvenile crime, the United States is in a league of its own.

Economist, *July 24, 1993*

Firearms and Youth Suicide

Most teen suicides are impulsive, spur of the moment acts. Youthful impatience and despair plus access to a lethal weapon create needless tragedies.

Every six hours, a pre-teen or teenager commits suicide with a gun—1,476 in all in 1990.

Guns are the leading method used by teenagers to commit suicide (60 percent).

The suicide rate of adolescents quadrupled between 1950 and 1988, making suicide the third leading cause of adolescent death.

The odds that potentially suicidal adolescents will kill themselves double when a gun is kept in the home.

An estimated 3.6 million high school students across the country considered taking their own lives in 1990.

"Youth Suicide Surveillance," Centers for Disease Control, 1990

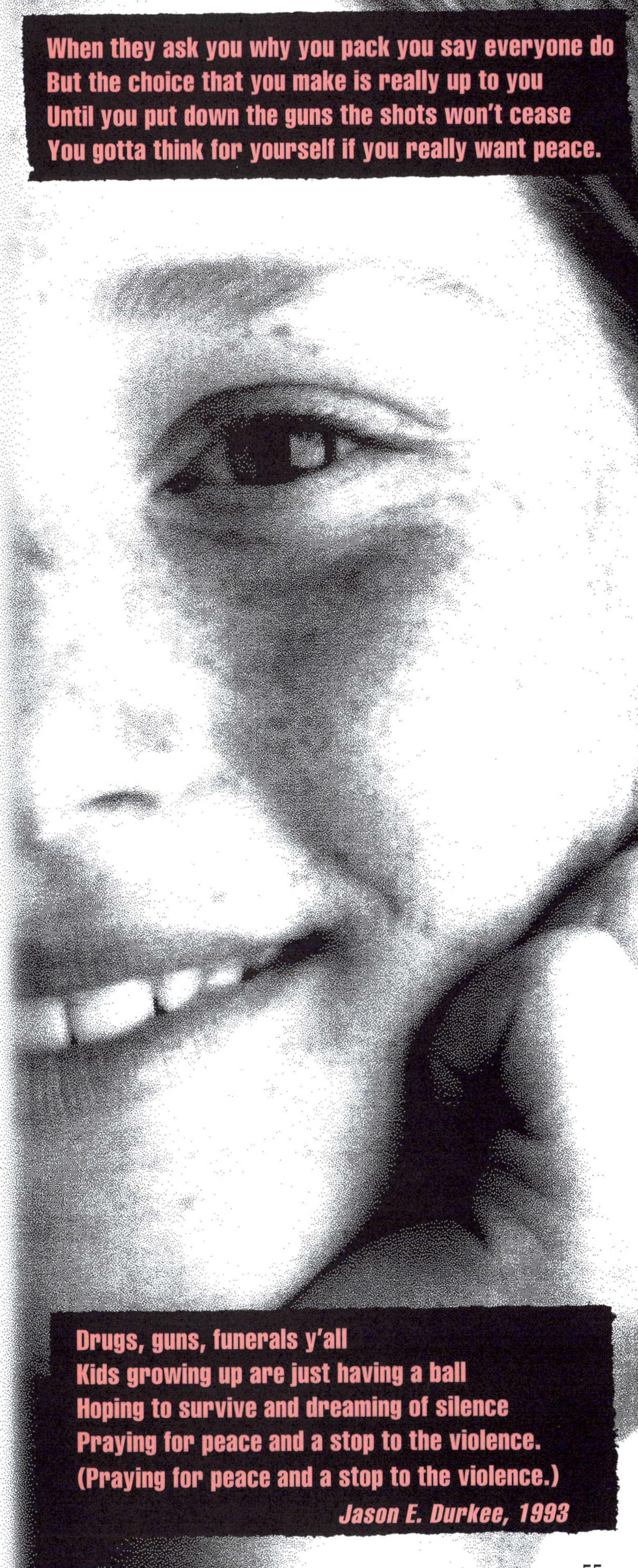

Photograph courtesy Conrad & Company

Ten Things Kids Can Do to Stop Violence

1 Settle arguments with words, not fists or weapons. Don't stand around and form an audience when others are arguing. A group makes a good target for violence.

2 Learn safe routes for walking in the neighborhood, and know good places to seek help. Trust feelings, and if there's a sense of danger, get away fast.

3 Report any crime or suspicious actions to the police, school authorities, and parents. Be willing to testify if needed.

4 Don't open the door to anyone you don't know and trust.

5 Never go anywhere with someone you don't know and trust.

6 If someone tries to abuse you, say no, get away, and tell a trusted adult. Remember, it's not the victim's fault.

7 Don't use alcohol or other drugs, and stay away from places and people associated with them.

8 Stick with friends who are also against violence and drugs, and stay away from known trouble spots.

9 Get involved to make school safer and better by having poster contests against violence, holding antidrug rallies, counseling peers, and settling disputes peacefully. If there's no program, help start one!

10 Help younger children learn to avoid being crime victims. Set a good example, and volunteer to help with community efforts to stop crime.

Tips courtesy of the National Crime Prevention Council, Washington, D.C.

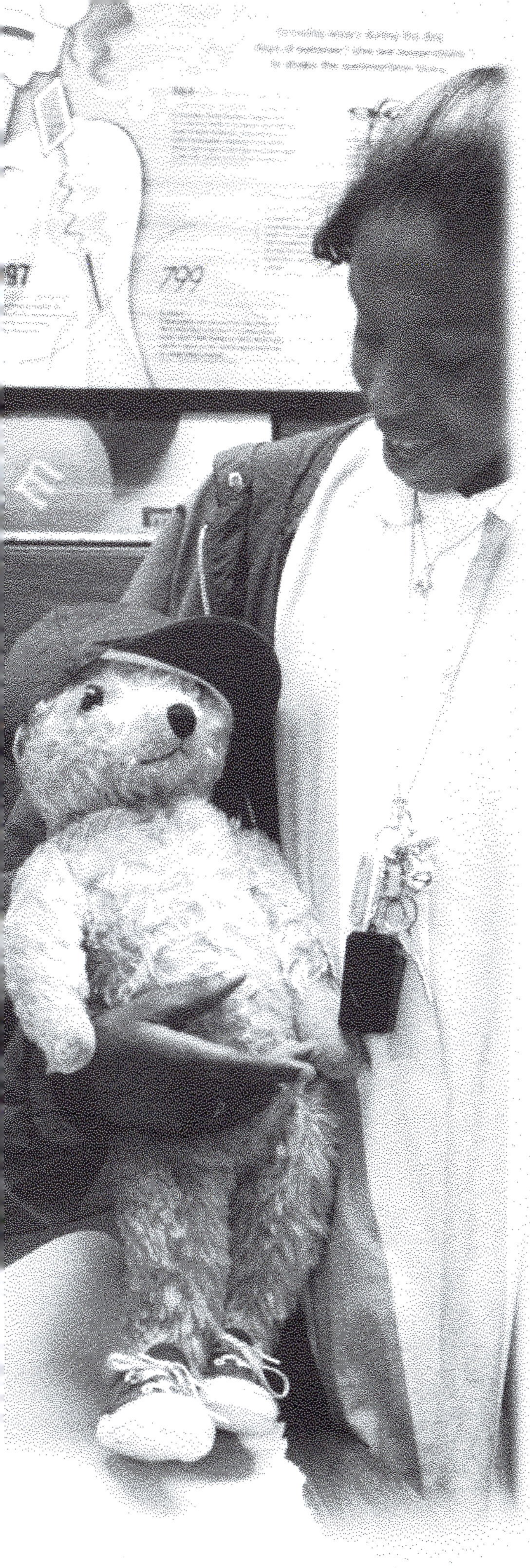

Nine Things Adults Can Do to Stop Violence

1 Teach children how to reduce their risk of being victims of violent crime. Insist on knowing where your kids are, what they are doing, and whom they are with.

2 Use common-sense tips to reduce your risk of being a crime victim. Stay in well-lighted, busy areas, travel with a friend if possible, and walk in a confident, assured way. Avoid known trouble spots.

3 Don't carry a weapon. You lose, whether you use it or it's used on you.

4 Report crimes and suspicious activities to police; agree to testify when necessary. Stand up for what you believe in if you want a safe community.

5 Get to know your neighbors and agree to look out for each other. Get organized. Work with the police.

6 Find ways to settle arguments without violence. If you resort to violence to settle disputes, a child may well follow your example. Be a good role model.

7 Don't support illegal activities, such as buying stolen property or using illegal drugs. It's the wrong message to send a child, and it involves you in criminal activity.

8 Use common courtesy. It helps ease tensions that can lead to violence. Teach your kids that good manners are important.

9 Get involved. Volunteer to help in community and neighborhood anticrime efforts. Encourage groups you belong to—religious, civic, social—to help stop crime.

Tips courtesy of the National Crime Prevention Council, Washington, D.C.

Reading List, Films, Organizations and Resources

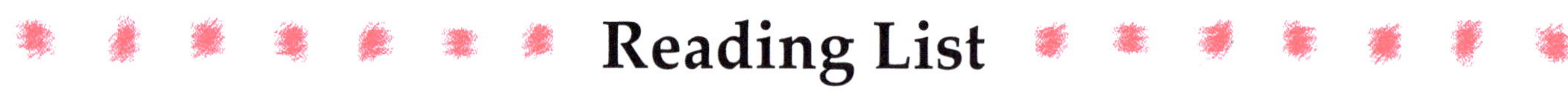

Reading List

Auletta, Ken. "The Electronic Parent: Annals of Communication."*New Yorker,* November 8, 1993.

Bing, Léon. *Do or Die.* New York: Harper Collins, 1992.

Brent, David A., et al. "The Presence and Accessibility of Firearms in the Homes of Adolescent Suicides: A Case-Control Study." *JAMA* (*Journal of the American Medical Association*), vol. 266, no. 21 (December 4, 1991). (For reprints, write to: Dr. David A. Brent, Services for Teens at Risk, Western Psychiatric Institute and Clinic, 3811 O'Hara St., Pittsburgh, PA 15213-2593)

Cartwright, Madeline, and Michael D'Orso. *For the Children: Lessons from a Visionary Principal.* New York: Doubleday, 1993.

Centerwall, Brandon S. "Exposure to Television as a Risk Factor for Violence." *American Journal of Epidemiology,* vol. 129, no. 4 (April 1989). (For reprints, write to: Dr. Brandon S. Centerwall, Dept. of Epidemiology, SC-36, University of Washington, Seattle, WA 98195)

Children's Express. *Voices from the Future: Our Children Speak About Violence in America.* Edited by Susan Goodwillie. New York: Crown Publishers, 1993.

Coles, Robert. *The Call of Service: A Witness to Idealism.* Boston: Houghton Mifflin, 1993.

———. *Children of Crisis, Vol. I: A Study of Courage and Fear*. Boston: Atlantic Little, Brown, 1977.

———. *The Moral Life of Children.* Boston: Little, Brown, 1986.

———. *The Political Life of Children.* Boston: Little, Brown, 1986.

Committee on Injury and Poison Prevention. "Firearm Injuries Afflicting the Pediatric Population." *Pediatrics,* vol. 89, no. 4 (April 1992).

Cotton, Paul. "Gun-Associated Violence Increasingly Viewed as Public Health Challenge." *JAMA,* vol. 267, no. 9 (March 4, 1992).

Donaldson, Greg. *The Ville: Cops and Kids in Urban America.* New York: Ticknor and Fields, 1993.

Fingerhut, Lois A. "Firearm Mortality Among Children, Youth, and Young Adults 1–34 Years of Age, Trends and Current Status: United States, 1985–90." Advance Data no. 231, Hyattsville, Md.: National Center for Health Statistics, Centers for Disease Control Prevention, 1993. (Write to: U.S. Dept. of Health and Human Services, 6525 Belcrest Rd., Hyattsville, MD 20782)

Ford, Clyde W. *We* Can *All Get Along: 50 Steps You Can Take to Help End Racism.* New York: Dell, 1994.

Goldsmith, Suzanne. *A City Year: On the Streets and in the Neighborhoods with Twelve Young Community Service Volunteers.* New York: New Press, 1993.

Goldstein, Arnold P., and C. Ronald Huff, eds. *The Gang Intervention Handbook.* Champaign, Ill.: Research Press, 1993.

Harrington, Walt. *Crossings: A White Man's Journey into Black America.* New York: Harper Collins, 1993.

Katz, John. "The Media's War on Kids: From the Beatles to Beavis and Butthead." *Rolling Stone,* November 25, 1993.

Kellerman, Arthur L., et al. "Suicide in the Home in Relation to Gun Ownership." *New England Journal of Medicine,* vol. 327, no. 7 (August 13, 1992).

Kotlowitz, Alex. *There Are No Children Here: The Story of Two Boys Growing Up in the Other America.* New York: Doubleday, 1992.

Kozol, Jonathan. *Death at an Early Age: The Destruction of the Minds and Hearts of Negro Children in the Boston Public Schools.* Boston: Houghton Mifflin, 1967.

———. *Rachel and Her Children: Homeless Families in America.* New York: Crown Publishers, 1988.

———. *Savage Inequalities: Children in America's Schools.* New York: Crown Publishers, 1991.

Larson, Erik. *Lethal Passage: How the Travels of a Single Handgun Expose the Roots of America's Gun Crisis.* New York: Crown Publishers, 1994.

———. "The Story of a Gun: The Maker, the Dealer, the Murderer: Inside the Out-of-Control World of American Firearms." *Atlantic,* January 1993.

McCall, Nathan. *Makes Me Wanna Holler: A Young Black Man in America.* New York: Random House, 1994.

Myers, Walter Dean. *Scorpions.* (A young adult novel about a boy, gangs, and a gun.) New York: Harper Collins, 1988.

Nightingale, Carl Husemoller. *On the Edge: A History of Poor Black Children and Their American Dreams.* New York: Basic Books, 1993.

"A Preliminary Assessment of Violence in Washington State." Washington State Department of Health, Injury Prevention Program, 1993.

Prothrow-Stith, Deborah, with Michaele Weissman. *Deadly Consequences: How Violence Is Destroying Our Teenage Population and a Plan to Begin Solving the Problem.* New York: Harper Collins, 1991.

Safran, Claire. "A Tale of Two Cities, and the Difference Guns Make." *Good Housekeeping,* November 1993.

Spergel, Irving A., and Robert L. Chance. "National Youth Gang Suppression and Intervention Program." National Institute of Justice Reports. Chicago: Office of Juvenile Justice and Delinquency Prevention, June 1991.

Sugarmann, Josh, and Kristen Rand. "Cease Fire." *Rolling Stone,* March 10, 1994.

———. *Cease Fire: A Comprehensive Strategy to Reduce Firearms Violence.* Violence Policy Center, Washington, D.C. Straight Arrow Publishers Company, L.P., 1994.

Williams, Terry, and William Kornblum. *The Uptown Kids: Struggle and Hope in the Projects.* New York: G. P. Putnam's Sons, 1994.

Films

Some of these films contain profanity and scenes of graphic violence and brutality. They are shocking, but even more shocking is that they reflect the reality facing many of America's children. Most of the teenagers I work with have seen these films and vouch for their authenticity.

American Me. Directed by Edward James Olmos. 1992.

Bound by Honor, or, *Blood in, Blood Out.* Directed by Taylor Hackford. 1993.

Boyz N the Hood. Directed by John Singleton. 1991.

I Am a Promise: The Children of Stanton Elementary School. Directed by Susan Raymond. 1993.

Lives in Hazard. Directed by Susan Todd and Andrew Young, 1993.

Menace II Society. Directed by Allen and Albert Hughes. 1993.

Stand and Deliver. Directed by Ramon Menendez. 1987.

Strapped. Directed by Forest Whitaker. 1993.

There Are No Children Here. Directed by Anita W. Addison. Based on a book by Alex Kotlowitz. 1993.

Organizations

Center to Prevent Handgun Violence
1225 Eye St. NW, Suite 1100
Washington, DC 20025
(202) 289-7319

Among the information available from the Center is the STAR Program (Straight Talk About Risks) for preschool through twelfth grade, which features values, decision-making, conflict resolution, safety, personal choices, anger management, and peer-pressure lessons to help students make better choices.

Children's Express News Service
1440 New York Ave. NW, Suite 510
Washington, DC 20005
(202) 73-PRESS

Founded in 1975, this service provides news reported and edited "by children for everyone." This is serious journalism with fresh and startling results.

Cities in Schools
401 Wythe St., Suite 200
Alexandria, VA 22314-1963
(703) 519-8999

1001 Fourth Ave. Plaza, Suite 3010
Seattle, WA 98154
(206) 461-8313

Founded in 1977, Cities in Schools (CIS, Inc.), a comprehensive nonprofit prevention program involving state and local communities with public schools, brings resources to children. Divisions of CIS include:

Powerful Schools
3301 S. Horton
Seattle, WA 98144
(206) 722-5543

Safe Haven
821 Second Ave., Suite 2110
Seattle, WA 98104
(206) 919-8412

A project that promotes mentorship and youth leadership.

MAVIA (Mothers Against Violence in America)
P.O. Box 444
Mercer Island, WA 98040

MAVIA works through community programs and education to reduce violence in our society and to promote the well being and safety of our children, and seeks legislation to keep guns out of the hands of children. Educational packages that give kids tools to handle conflict without violence are available.

Mothers Against Police Harassment
P.O. Box 22886
Seattle, WA 98122
(206) 329-2033

This group informs citizens of the code of conduct expected of officers and establishes a code of conduct for children in the presence of police. It holds workshops to support children in modifying behavior.

SAVE (Students Against Violence Everywhere)
Gary Weart, Advisor
West Charlotte High School
2219 Senior Dr.
Charlotte, NC 28216
(704) 343-6060

This student-initiated program has a long-range, proactive approach. Students work with students to deliver a message of nonviolence and promote conflict resolution, gun safety and awareness, and what to do if confronted by a gun. These students believe they can make a difference and have established guidelines and a constitution which they encourage others to share. With an annual two dollar membership fee they have founded a $500 scholarship in memory of student Alex Orange, a victim of gun violence.

Seattle Youth Involvement Network
107 Cherry St., 5th Floor
Seattle, WA 98104
(206) 461-8524

Kids six to twenty-one are eligible to join this group which seeks to empower and involve young people in their community. Projects and events reflect the goal of creating a "Kids Place" city. Government and private agencies as well as youth advocacy groups are part of the network. ABSA (All Brothers and Sisters Allowed) (206-461-8524) is a subgroup that uses theatrical skills to teach leadership, discipline, and self-esteem.

Second Step
172 20th Ave.
Seattle, WA 98122
(206) 322-5050

A violence-prevention program committee for children, Second Step offers a preschool–eighth grade curriculum consisting of photographs and lesson cards.

Violence Policy Center
1300 N Street NW
Washington, DC 20005
(202) 783-4071

Founded in 1988, this group works to educate the public and promote understanding of the threat of the uncontrolled (teddy bears and toasters have tougher safety standards) gun industry, a branch of Big Business.

Washington Cease Fire
P.O. Box 15644
Seattle, WA 98115-0644
(206) 322-7564

This network of citizens and organizations works to promote health and safety by preventing violence, especially gun violence.

Wholistic Stress Control Institute, Inc.
P.O. Box 42481
Atlanta, GA 30311
(404) 344-2021

Positive ways to reduce anger are presented in educational materials for sixth–twelfth grade and a stress-control curriculum for kindergarten–fifth grade.

SEATTLE AREA RESOURCES

Remember, the neighborhood is a resource.

Get out of the house. Talk to your neighbor.
Go into another neighborhood. Join forces.
Hand in hand. Heart to heart.

The organizations, services, and projects listed here serve a broad spectrum of the Seattle community. I encourage readers elsewhere to look for similar services in your area. You may want to call a Seattle number to inquire about how a group works, and start a like organization or a "sister" group.

Your local police department is a good resource. The Seattle Police Department has programs and officers who are assigned to community outreach and education programs, such as the gang intervention unit and the D.A.R.E. (Drug Abuse Resistance Education) program. Officers lecture in schools and answer questions about law enforcement protocol, drug and gang resistance, and how to act if stopped by the police.

Reach out. Be creative. Energy makes energy. Involve kids. Talk with kids, not at them. Listen to what they say and include them in as many ways as possible. Pay attention.

The future is now !

(Area code 206)

African American School	281-6755
Asian Counseling and Referral Service	461-3606
Atlantic Street Center	329-2050
Bellevue Boys and Girls Club	465-6162
Big Brothers of King County	461-3630
Big Sisters of King County	461-8502
Boys and Girls Club of King County	461-3890
Boy Scouts of America	725-5200
Campfire Girls and Boys	461-8550
Catholic Community Services Refugee Assistance Program	323-9450
Catholic Youth Organization	382-4562
Central Area Motivation Program (multiservice organization serving the African American Community)	329-4111
Central Area Youth Association (mentorship consortium recruiting African American mentors)	322-6640
Children's Home Society	524-6020
Chinese Information and Service Center	624-0484
Christian Life Assembly	838-7522
Church Council of Greater Seattle	525-1213
Community Campership Program (American Red Cross camping opportunities for low-income children)	323-2345
Consejo Counseling and Referral Services	461-4880
El Centro de la Raza (multiservice center for the Chicano/Latino community)	329-2974
Filipino Youth Activities	461-4870
Four-H Program	296-3900
Girl Scouts	633-5600
Head Start Program	386-1001
Indochina Chinese Refugee Association	625-9955
International District Housing and Social Services	623-5132

Japanese Community Service	323-0250
Junior Achievement (an opportunity for students to learn business principles)	296-2600
Korean Community Counseling Center	784-5691
Lutheran Social Services	672-6009
Mount Zion Baptist Church	322-6500
Neighborhood House (social services for residents of public housing communities)	461-8430
Pacific Islander Children and Youth Services	722-9495
Parents Anonymous	233-0139 (1-800-932-HOPE)
Plymouth Congregational Church	622-4865
POCAAN (People of Color Against AIDS Network)	322-7061
PTA of Washington	565-2153
Puget Sound Blood Program	292-6500
Rainer Beach High School, Student Conflict Management Council (Rick Harwood)	281-6184
Refugee Women's Alliance	721-0243
ROPE (Rites of Passage Experience [CAMP]) (cultural values, orientation, career exploration, community service)	726-9572
Safe Streets Project, Tacoma	272-6824
Samoan Intervention and Resources	722-9495
Seattle Indian Health Board, Thunderbird (ages 12–17)	722-7152
Seattle Neighborhood Group (consults with communities on fighting crime)	728-0903
Seattle Parks Department (late-night and weekend programs for youth and teens; Reco Bembry)	684-7136
Seattle Police Department, Community Crime Prevention	684-7727
Seattle Public Schools, general information	281-6000
Seattle Urban League	461-3792
South Pacific Islander Dropout Prevention Program	281-6528
Stop the Violence, Commission on African-American Affairs (James Kelly)	753-0127
Stop the Violence, Seattle's Anti-Violence Project (Dale Tiffany, Dorothy Mann)	684-4507
STRIVE (Starting Teenage Responsibility in a Video Environment) (Tacoma teens produce documentaries on community issues)	572-7709
Union Gospel Mission (community youth computer program, drop-in center, and other after-school activities)	723-0767
United Indians of All Tribes, I-Wa-Sil Youth Home (ages 12–21)	781-8303
Vietnamese Friendship Association	323-9365
YMCA Job Center	382-5011
YMCA of Greater Seattle	382-5003
YouthCare (serving youth in crisis)	622-5555
Zion Preparatory Academy	322-2926

RESOURCES IN YOUR COMMUNITY

Neighborhood churches are a great resource.

It takes a whole village to raise a child.

African proverb

Postscript

Before I send this book to press I want to thank all the people who so generously and willingly helped make the poster and book a reality, beginning with the students at Whitworth Elementary School and a teacher, Mamie Robeson, and ending with the final dotting of an "i" by junior editors Heidi and Leif Petersen. I want to shout the names of all who made this project work: Stephen Pannone, Virginia Sabado, Tim Girvin and Tim Girvin Design, Marsha and Michael Burns, Joe Grande and Wescan Color Corporation, Jim Wheat and The Paper Zone, Mike Fitzgerald and K/P Corporation, Janet Jones, Gretchen Smyth and du Jour, Argentum Photo Service, Jason and Norman Durkee, Peter Riches, Detective Steve O'Leary, Lt. Emett Kelsie, Judge Michael S. Hurtado, Juanita Ramos, Kathy Footer and Harborview Medical Center, Janet Skeels, Jennifer Ricards and Puget Sound Blood Center, Madeline Wilde, Willie Redman, Michael Longyear, Harriet Walden, Blackbird Books, M Coy Books, Jenny Wieland, Ed Marquand and Marquand Books, Jo David and Jo David Art and Design, Patrick Soden, Lorri Hagman, Nelly Myhre, Shirley Collins, Sara and Louis Nawrot, Bruce Nordstrom, Wayne Wilson and US Bancorp Securities, Bagley Wright, Jean Falls, Camille Uhlir, Mary Coney, The Ruins, Llewelyn Pritchard, Mai and Wah Lui, Yuen Lui Studios, James Kelly, Teens on Target from Los Angeles, Ted Howard, Cleveland High School Portable No. 14 Council, Fia Faletogo, Tom Nakao, Ron Bolton, Domico Curry, Troy Lewis, and Naomi Roberson.

We all want to make the violence stop. Help us make peace the cool thing. We can do it. Starting right now.

Man did not weave the web of life, he is merely a strand in it. Whatever he does to the web, he does to himself.

Chief Seattle